The Quest for Meaningful
Special Education

The Quest for Meaningful Special Education

Amy Ballin

ROWMAN & LITTLEFIELD
Lanham • Boulder • New York • London

Published by Rowman & Littlefield
A wholly owned subsidiary of The Rowman & Littlefield Publishing Group, Inc.
4501 Forbes Boulevard, Suite 200, Lanham, Maryland 20706
www.rowman.com

Unit A, Whitacre Mews, 26-34 Stannary Street, London SE11 4AB

British Library Cataloguing in Publication Information Available

Library of Congress Cataloging-in-Publication Data

Names: Ballin, Amy, 1959-
Title: The quest for meaningful special education / Amy Ballin.
Description: Lanham, Maryland : Rowman & Littlefield, 2016. | Includes bibliographical references
    and index.
Identifiers: LCCN 2016049705 (print) | LCCN 2016051710 (ebook) | ISBN 9781475827583 (cloth :
    alk. paper) | ISBN 9781475827590 (pbk. : alk. paper) | ISBN 9781498527606 (Electronic)
Subjects: LCSH: Dyslexic children--Education--United States. | Private schools--United States.
Classification: LCC LC4708.5 .B34 2016 (print) | LCC LC4708.5 (ebook) | DDC 371.9--dc23
LC record available at https://lccn.loc.gov/2016049705

Printed in the United States of America

To the students and families at the Kelsey School, my family (Tim, Casey, Aaron, and Michael), my mother, Alice Ballin, and in memory of my father, Bert Ballin.

Contents

Preface

My Personal Educational Journey

In fourth grade, I got a "D" in spelling. In sixth grade, I realized I was the only student in my grade who had not published anything in the school newspaper, despite my earnest efforts to produce quality writing. In seventh grade, the entire class broke out laughing as I mispronounced the word "deny" while reading out loud. In eighth grade, I was placed in the remedial English class—what everyone referred to as "spelling for dummies"—with four other students. In ninth grade, my parents hired an after-school reading tutor. I have no memory of how or whether this tutoring helped. All I remember is that I was labeled as having a reading problem and needing extra help.

Clear messages throughout my schooling showed me that reading and writing were subjects to avoid at all costs, as I appeared unable to progress in these areas. In high school, I requested the lower-track English and history classes even while taking the highest-level classes in math and science. To avoid any English or foreign-language requirements, I chose to attend an agricultural college where most of the academic requirements complemented my strengths in math and science. After undergraduate school, I pursued my interests in science and education, choosing carefully a graduate school without a thesis requirement.

Despite my strengths in math and science, my straight-A grades in high school, and my admittance to an Ivy League university, the messages and labels in elementary and middle school that defined me as a slow reader and poor writer continued to scar me even in adulthood, dictating the choices I made and the things I avoided. I had a variety of coping strategies: scribbling my writing when I did not know how to spell a word, asking a participant to write on the easel when giving a workshop for teachers, and developing a debilitating cough when asked to read aloud.

My educational journey steered me away from ever working on my areas of weakness and, instead, channeled me toward my strengths in science and math. Because I had a keen interest in education and in working with teachers, I still had fantasies of earning my doctorate, but I feared that my difficulties with writing and my slow reading would make it impossible. It took me twenty years to gain the confidence to enter a doctoral program.

MY PASSION FOR THIS BOOK

I still remember my own fourth-grade in-class reading assignment on Homer's *Iliad.* The teacher instructed our class to read a passage to ourselves and then individually tell her how we understood the reading. Once finished, we could go out for recess. I never made it to recess. I read the passage over and over again, watching out of the corner of my eye as every other child headed out to recess. I could make no sense of what I read. That incident, and many similar ones, shaped my low self-confidence in reading and writing.

My grade school report cards suggest a student who today might be diagnosed with dyslexia. As early as first grade, my teacher reported, "Phonics sometimes holds her back from analyzing and spelling new words." My second-grade teacher described my "hesitancy in verbal subjects" and noted that I was reading below grade level. This teacher suggested that my reading would improve as I gained confidence in skills such as phonics and spelling.

By third grade, my teacher noted, "Amy is plagued by persistent reversals of letters and letter combinations. This makes it especially difficult for her to develop a sight feeling for words." In fourth grade, letter grades appeared on my report card along with comments. I earned a C- in spelling, and the teacher commented that the word reversals were disappearing. In fifth grade, my teacher questioned whether there might be a problem with my eyes, as he noted "a mixing of the order of letters and uncertainty of final syllables of words" and commented on my difficulties in reading and writing.

Comments continued along the same lines as I made my way through school with difficulties in spelling and then in writing. No one identified a reading disability until ninth grade, when limited help was finally implemented.

My story dates back forty years, to the early stages of research on reading and the understanding of dyslexia. Yet even today, although researchers have made tremendous gains in the field, stories similar to mine continue. Both Shaywitz (2003) and Wolf (2007) describe their frustrations with school personnel's lack of knowledge and understanding of reading disabilities.

Many successful adults can describe their humiliation at being identified as poor readers during their school years. Olson (2009) notes numerous examples of students with learning disabilities who have been wounded by experiences in school. Wolf (2007) describes Grand Prix racing driver Jackie Stewart's lifelong feelings of damage as a result of his childhood embarrassment at being a poor reader. Stewart indicated that he would have ended up in jail had he not found success in race car driving.

In fact, many struggling readers do end up in jail. Research suggests that individuals with learning disabilities are overrepresented in the U.S. prison population. For example, in a study of fifty inmates in a Texas prison, Moody et al. (2000) discovered that the prisoners were twice as likely as the general population to have difficulty with single-word decoding—defined by these authors as the "core component of dyslexia" (p. 69).

In a study of Swedish juvenile prisons, Svensson, Lundberg, and Jacobson (2001) claim a well-documented association between reading disabilities and juvenile delinquency. They found that more than two-thirds of young offenders had difficulties with written language.

Grigorenko, et al. (2015) also found evidence that the rate of learning disabilities in the juvenile prison population was twice that of the general population. They acknowledge the variety of definitions of learning disability complicating research on this topic. They suggest using the term "deficient academic performance" (p. 364). Using this definition, they claim, makes it very clear that the population of juvenile offenders underperform academically compared to the general population.

Snowling et al. (2000) found that the rate of dyslexia in the prison population (based on their own testing) mirrored the rate in the nonincarcerated population. They concur, however, that high levels of literacy problems exist among young offenders. They suggest that major factors contributing to low literacy rates are poor school attendance, inadequate educational opportunities, and lack of interest in school. Perhaps the precise label "dyslexia" is less important than the fact that the prison population appears to have a higher proportion of struggling readers than the nonincarcerated population.

Moody et al. (2000) suggest that "poor performance in school or at work too often leads to a life of crime and eventual imprisonment" (p. 69), but they clarify that dyslexia is not the cause of the criminal behavior. Rather, they propose that lack of attention to the struggling reader likely leads to emotional despair. They explain that the experience of unremediated dyslexia becomes an "emotionally degrading life for the dyslexic child, who is often being told how lazy he is when he knows how hard he has been trying" (p. 74).

Grigorenko et al. (2015) note the research on adults with deficient academic skills clearly shows a connection with unemployment, depression, and higher rates of substance abuse, which mirrors common issues with the prison population.

Kirk and Reid (2001) note that without remediation, students are more likely to develop low self-worth, which "predisposes young people to offend" (p. 83). The common phrases "schoolhouse to jailhouse" (Ferris, 2015) and "pipeline to prison" (Mader & Butrymowicz, 2014) reflect the failure of our schools to provide a meaningful education for many young people—especially the special-education population, who account for 70 percent of juvenile prisoners. With the exorbitant cost to house juvenile prisoners perhaps this money could be better spent helping children learn to read, with less emphasis on labeling students and more emphasis on providing support.

Moody et al. (2000) state, "Teaching everyone to read is not a utopian dream but a realistic goal for which no shortcuts exist. As for cost, the more relevant question is whether we can afford not to do it" (p. 74). Former U.S. Secretary of Education Arne Duncan, in a June 2012 press release, stated, "Encouraging students to improve their reading is a key to their success in school and in life." Although I agree that learning to read is essential, based on the stories recounted in this book, it does not appear that children need encouragement as much as they need correct instruction and the appropriate environment.

For struggling readers, the result can be low self-confidence, as happened in my own case, which can influence later choices. In some cases, the consequences are more severe—at the extreme, perhaps a life of crime that may result in imprisonment. Regardless of the extent of the consequences, the experiences of struggling readers may have a major effect on decisions they make later in life.

MISGUIDED SCHOOL REFORMS AND THE INFLUENCE OF CULTURE

Improving education for all students is not a new concept. New educational reforms continually emerge, usually as the result of a perceived educational crisis that leads to the imposition of new regulations and to the passage of legislation designed to improve schools. Yet the achievement gap, also referred to as the opportunity gap (Oakes et al., 2014), persists (Lee, 2002), and not all students learn to read. Many educational researchers note that reform efforts have largely ignored the influences on student learning of school culture, as well as cultural influences from outside the school, and demonstrate the many ways in which these influences affect how students learn in school (Deal & Peterson, 1990, 1999; Renchler, 1992). I agree.

Studying school culture requires an examination of noncurricular aspects of school life. In this book, I explore the relationship of school culture to student learning. I am interested not only in the culture that exists within the school itself but also in the ways in which larger cultural influences outside the school inform the school culture and determine the ways in which schools operate. The area I explore in depth is the role of the construction of special education and how this construction may deter many students from gaining access to the kind of education that will facilitate learning to read.

A SURPRISING DISCOVERY

It was with great surprise that I came to understand my own learning issues through the process of researching these students' educational journeys. Like the students described in this book, I discovered my learning issues in a serendipitous fashion. I feel compassion for the students who appear in this book and for others in the same situation, as I am in a good position to understand the labels, limitations, and expectations that others place on us and that we also place on ourselves.

It was this passion that drove my research. As was common years ago and is still the case for many students today, my learning issues were not identified or addressed until later in my educational career. Even then, I probably never received appropriate services that would have directly addressed and remediated my language disability. The same is true for many adults and children today, who may have never understood that their struggles with language were not related to intelligence and, in fact, could be remediated.

This information deserves more attention, as does the undue suffering of so many schoolchildren who are unable to access the education provided, often as the result of labels that prevent them from getting the education they deserve. Through the stories presented in this book, I hope to draw attention to these children and to demonstrate how one school's model might point the way to a possible solution.

Acknowledgments

I am grateful to the numerous people who supported, taught, guided, and encouraged me throughout this journey. Without them, I would not have achieved my goal.

My childhood friend, Dr. Reverend Traci C. West, provided the inspiration for me to pursue a doctorate and to write this book. She supported me through every step of the process.

Four special people, who are not only great friends but also excellent writers, Kiki Zeldes, Martha Morgan, Pat Baker, and Tara Gallagher, provided editorial advice throughout this process, as well as emotional support and encouragement.

My children, Casey, Aaron, and Michael, asked probing questions about my work, understood when I was not home for dinner, and most importantly provided technical computer support whenever needed.

My parents, Alice Ballin and Dr. Bert Ballin, encouraged me from the start of my educational career. They provided many opportunities for me to learn and supported me both financially and emotionally.

I owe tremendous gratitude to my husband, Tim Greiner, who gave me the space and time needed to complete this project along with the support to guide me through this process. He is my best friend, my partner, and my cheerleader in my pursuits of my professional career.

Dr. Caroline Heller, my committee chair and faculty advisor, not only held me to high standards but she also helped me find my direction. It was Caroline who suggested following the educational journey of individual students. It was with this focus that I fell in love with my topic and tuned into my own dyslexia. Caroline's guidance along the way kept me going. Her encouragement, with even the most simplistic phrases such as "I think you are on the right track," inspired me to keep at it.

Finally, this book would not have been possible without the many participants from the Kelsey School who shared with me their stories and expertise. I want to thank the teachers and administrators who took time out of their busy schedule to meet with me and also allowed me to observe their classroom. I especially want to acknowledge Raya, James, Mike, Evette, and Frank, the five children who endured me following them to classes and, along with Nancy, relived their painful educational journeys. I also appreciate all the parents who gave up time to interview with me, shared their personal records, and gave me permission to work with their child. They, like their children, relived many painful memories in the telling of their child's story.

I am thankful to have the support of all the people who helped in various ways along my own educational journey.

Introduction

-

For a full 20 percent of school-age children, learning to read is an arduous task that, depending on multiple factors—including luck, socioeconomic status, race, residence, and parent advocacy—may or may not result in success. This book explores common themes from the educational journeys of nine students with language-based learning disabilities (LBLD) who found their way to a school that specializes in teaching to them, inclusive of their disabilities.

The school, referred to as the Kelsey School, is a model that works for students with LBLD. According to the Learning Disabilities Association of America, 38.7 percent of U.S. students with learning disabilities drop out of high school—double the rate of students without learning disabilities. At Kelsey, 100 percent of the students graduate and, on average, 93 percent go on to college.

The educational journeys of these six students and three parents highlight the inequities in the educational system and raise questions about the meaning of an accessible education. The students described in this book were underdiagnosed, misdiagnosed, and—at times—overdiagnosed with a variety of labels. This labeling, required in order to qualify for specialized instruction, determined each child's pathway through the educational system—a pathway with consequences that, at times, appeared to hinder rather than support the child's academic progress.

This labeling process represents just one of the many concerns associated with the construction of special education. The students and their families also endured financial and emotional hardships in their fight to obtain an accessible education. These hardships raise questions about the ethics of current educational practices.

The children described in this story arrived at the Kelsey School at different times, depending on their individual stories, but all of them began attending Kelsey between 2004 and 2008. At Kelsey, for the first time, they experienced an education that matched their learning needs, allowing them to progress both academically and emotionally. They went from feeling despair about themselves and their academic skills to finding self-confidence in their abilities, both academic and social. They also experienced the profound satisfaction of learning to read. This positive school environment was a new experience for these children.

The Kelsey School's structure, supportive learning environment, and dedicated staff create a collaborative school culture that supports successful student learning. This book describes this model and highlights the ways in which staff, students, and parents all contribute to its success.

The evidence presented in this book validates the hard reality that only a limited number of children are fortunate enough to obtain this privileged education. For those who do not, the consequences are potentially dire. Struggling readers typically experience low self-confidence and poor academic performance. For some, the consequences are more severe. Adolescents with reading difficulties have a higher rate of suicide, and a disproportionate number of prison inmates struggle with reading. Yet current research shows that most struggling readers, given the right environment, can learn to read.

This book questions the efficacy of special education, provides new meaning to the concept of "access to education," and explores the ways in which the current special education model supports deficit thinking (defined as a focus on children's academic challenges rather than their strengths) that may do more harm than good. Not all children have the opportunity to attend a school that specializes in teaching to their disability. What happens to those who do not? How have special education programs, designed to meet the needs of students with learning disabilities, failed the very students they are supposed to help? In particular, given the current research on teaching reading, why are so many students still struggling with reading in schools?

These are some of the questions raised in this book. The book will expose some of the problems with the current special education system and will also provide a successful model that can give hope to those stuck in similar circumstances.

Kelsey serves students identified as having language-based learning disabilities. Common among these students are tumultuous schooling experiences that led to low self-esteem and poor motivation. Once they started at the Kelsey School, the students experienced dramatic changes. One student noted, "We are all the same here and do not have to feel stupid." Another student described her feeling of being at home once she started at Kelsey.

ABOUT THE STUDENTS AND PARENTS

All of the students and parents have been given pseudonyms to protect their identity.

The central students in the book include the following:

- **Raya** and her mother, Mel
- **Evette** and her mother, Barbara
- **Nancy** and her mother, Libby
- **Frank** and his mother, Ella
- **James** and his mother, Mia, and father, Peter
- **Mike** and his mother, Evelyn

These students all came to the Kelsey School at different ages. Their stories were recorded in 2009, when they were middle school students.

Several additional parents also talk about their children:

- **Lesley**, who describes issues that arose for her daughter Polly
- **Mary**, who passionately describes her struggles getting Beth to Kelsey
- **Debbie**, whose three children—Callie, Tim, and Robert—have all been diagnosed with LBLD

All teachers and staff members have been given pseudonyms to protect their identity as well as different job titles in some cases.

KELSEY SCHOOL TEACHERS AND ADMINISTRATORS

Administration:

- Bert Stack, Principal
- Allison Tripp, Academic Administrator
- Sean Richner, Dean of Students
- Paul Standard, Public school liaison

Department Heads:

- Claire Jenkens
- Patrick Steel

Student Advisors:

- Sally McKay
- Kelly Dance

- Anna Brush
- Erin Stout

Veteran Teachers:

- Fiona Manner
- Patty Ryer

First-Year Teacher:

- Maggie Wright

Admissions:

- Lynn Kamer

Founder:

- Anthony Black

ABOUT THE KELSEY SCHOOL

The Kelsey School is a pseudonym for a private school that serves students in grades 2 through 12. Although Kelsey is considered a private school, approximately 50 percent of its students are publicly funded through the referring district school. The other 50 percent pay tuition. The Kelsey School is distinctive both in the population it serves and in its approach to learning. The school enrolls only students with language-based learning disabilities, including those with dyslexia as well as students with difficulties in written and oral expression.

Kelsey defines the term *language-based learning disability* broadly, to encompass both oral- and written-language difficulties, which include *writing/speaking* (formulation, organization, word retrieval), *reading/spelling,* and *listening/comprehending.* The school does not accept students with emotional, social, or behavioral issues.

CHAPTER DESCRIPTIONS

Part I: A Broken System

Part I contains four chapters that together describe the pain, frustrations, and inequities that some students experience in the process of trying to find an accessible education. The historical development of the system of special education further unravels the meaning behind an accessible education.

Chapter 1: Unexpected Consequences

This chapter describes the unintended consequences that these students encountered as they entered the public school system. The students and parents recall painful stories of their experiences and reveal the complex coping strategies they used to deal with the embarrassment and hardship of attending school with a learning disability. All students should have equal access to an education. Yet, this chapter tells the personal stories of some children with learning disabilities who have been denied that access.

Chapter 2: Special Education: How Did We Get Here?

This chapter calls into question the values at the heart of "special education," challenging readers to consider how an educational approach originally designed to help some of the neediest learners may instead disadvantage them for life. The commonly used deficit model of special education is explored, along with inequities in how dyslexia is diagnosed.

Chapter 3: The Serendipitous Pathway

Securing an education that works for your child should be easy. Unfortunately, for too many families, it isn't. Yet these families describe common experiences in their quest to understand their child's academic struggles and find a school that meets the child's needs. The parents used their instincts to reject what they heard from professionals; they learned how to interpret their child's behavior; they found someone who knew about Kelsey; and they educated themselves on dyslexia and special-education law. Finally, they lost faith in their public school's ability to meet their child's educational needs and pulled their child out. It is through this arduous and circuitous pathway that the families found their way to the Kelsey School.

Chapter 4: Measures of Success

This chapter describes how both the students and the parents evaluated the success of the Kelsey School approach. Individual success was measured not by test scores but instead by how students felt about themselves, how successful they were at achieving academic independence, and how socially successful they were.

Part II: The Kelsey School: A Model That Works

Part II presents the aspects of the Kelsey School that make it successful from the perspectives of the students, their parents, and a sample of the staff. Each chapter describes a theme that contributes to the overall functioning of the school. These themes, taken together, create a learning environment that appears to work for these students.

Chapter 5: Dedication to the Mission

In this chapter, the staff's dedication to the mission of the school emerges as a driving force behind the success of the school. The Kelsey staff community rallies around the mission. The common core values that are espoused in the mission appear as the glue that keeps the staff all working toward a common goal.

Chapter 6: The People Method

This chapter highlights the "people method," which Bert Stack described as the key to Kelsey's success. Bert coined this phrase in response to visitors who asked what methods Kelsey uses to make so many students successful. The "people method" allows for specific programming such as the use of the recitation, the student advisor, and small class size.

Chapter 7: Teachers as Learners

Chapter 7 describes how teacher-learning opportunities are institutionalized at Kelsey to provide ongoing teacher education. Learning opportunities for teachers are woven into the fabric of the school. This strong foundation enables the school to hire inexperienced teachers while also maintaining the knowledge and expertise of their veteran teachers.

Chapter 8: A Carefully Selected Population, a Consistent Academic Structure

In chapter 8, the admissions director outlines the highly selective process that is used to find students who are a good match for the teaching expertise of Kelsey's faculty and the academic structure of the school's program. A detailed exploration of the academic structure describes the consistency, routine, and systems that make the academic environment work for students from this carefully selected population.

Chapter 9: Communication at Kelsey

Chapter 9 describes a unique institutionalized communication system that enables Kelsey's teachers, students, and parents to access one another in a consistent and reliable fashion. The daily Snack Time meeting along with specialized report cards and a community message board allow communication in multiple venues and forms.

Chapter 10: A Supportive Community

In Chapter 10, Kelsey staff, students, and parents note the importance of a supportive school environment. They describe the specific ways in which mutual support is intrinsic to Kelsey at every level, from administration to student body.

Chapter 11: Safety at Kelsey

Chapter 11 highlights the feeling of safety and trust that students describe at Kelsey. The chapter identifies myriad ways in which the students feel this safety—a forgiving classroom environment, a sense of connection with other students who share the same learning challenges, and a close and trusting relationship with their teachers.

Chapter 12: Drawbacks and Privileges

No school contains the perfect model, and Kelsey is no exception. Chapter 12 focuses on some of Kelsey's drawbacks, as recorded by teachers and parents, including low pay for teachers and frustrations with space needs. In addition, this chapter highlights aspects of this privileged private-school environment that could become part of every public school.

Part III: The Change That Is Possible: Every Child Can Succeed

This third part contains the final chapter of the book. This chapter highlights ways in which all children can share in the model and the privileged education available to students at the Kelsey School.

Chapter 13: A New Vision for Educating All Children

This final chapter explores the social and political ramifications of an educational system that denies some students access to an education. It challenges current thinking about "normal" and "abnormal" (or "typical" and "special needs") children and suggests that, instead, all students are better served when treated as individuals with unique strengths and weakness. The chapter closes with ideas for changes schools can make in their quest to educate all children.

Part I

A Broken System

"It is just terrible how a child has to suffer and a parent has to spend thousands of dollars to prove a child needs help." (Mary, May 2009)

"I strongly believe that behind the success of every disabled child is a passionately committed, intensely engaged, and totally empowered parent, usually but not always the child's mother." (Shaywitz, 2003, p. 9)

Chapter One

Unexpected Consequences

Many children enter school ready and eager to learn. Parents enroll their children trusting that the school system has hired teachers and administrators that have the knowledge and expertise to meet their child's learning needs and that policy makers have created laws that support a child's learning. Mary went along with the school system when they recommended mainstreaming her daughter Beth and decreasing her pullout time. Mary trusted that the system knew what was best for her daughter, only to find years later that Beth had been denied an education. "Now, all this time, I'm . . . ignorant beyond belief. I had no idea." Mary and Beth are not alone. For the nine students featured in this book, schooling had unexpected consequences.

Most of the students in this book stayed in public schools after receiving a diagnosis of dyslexia, but eventually their parents realized that the public school system was failing to educate their child. Some reached this conclusion sooner than others. For example, one mother, Mel, removed her daughter, Raya, from the public school even before the school had developed an Individualized Education Plan (IEP). Other parents kept children in the system and tried to make it work, without fully realizing what they would need to know in order to accomplish this. Although the children left their public schools at different ages, they shared many of the same experiences as they struggled to get an education.

The children's and family's reactions to the special education programs of "pullout" and "mainstream" contradicted the intent of these programs. The students experienced blame because of their disability. Both the parents and the children suffered emotional hardships and the parents underwent financial challenges. These consequences culminated in both the child and the parent developing counterproductive strategies to cope with the pain of trying to navigate school with a learning disability.

3

PULLOUT AND MAINSTREAMING

With the enactment of the Education for All Handicapped Children Act of 1975 (PL 94-142), the concept of educating special education students in the least restrictive environment that could meet their educational needs emerged (Salend, 2016). Terms such as *pullout, mainstreaming, push-in,* and *inclusion* refer to the different venues schools use to meet this requirement. Before the enactment of this law, over 1 million students with disabilities were denied a public education and if they were in the public schools, they were often segregated. Since the enactment of this law, students have gained better access to public education. This law was the predecessor to the current Individuals with Disabilities Education Act (IDEA), 2004 (Salend, 2016).

In pullout programs, students leave the general education classroom and spend a portion of the day in a resource room with a special education teacher, as determined by their IEP. Special education teachers provide individualized instruction in specific skills to a small group of students with learning disabilities. They may also provide supplemental instruction that supports the instruction students receive in the general education classroom (Salend, 1990, 2016).

Pullout is used in conjunction with mainstreaming. Salend (2016) suggests that although *mainstreaming* and *inclusion* have been used interchangeably, they can also be seen as distinctive terms. *Mainstreaming* implies that students might spend some of their day in a separate special education classroom and will be included in the general education classroom for some of the day; the amount of time spent in each depends on the child's readiness for the main classroom environment. Typically, students might join the general education population for subjects such as art, physical education, music, and perhaps science and social studies, but will spend some of their day in the special education resource room for math and language arts (Schwarz, 2006).

The inclusion model, by contrast, is designed to keep special education students in the general education classroom, with classroom support, differentiated instruction, and curriculum adaptations. The parents and children in this story used the term *mainstreaming* more commonly than *inclusion,* although neither parents nor children ever distinguish between the two. Salend (2016) suggests that the term *inclusion* is currently replacing the term *mainstreaming.*

Many students featured in this book disliked being pulled out of their regular classroom to go to a resource room. They felt embarrassment about being pulled out, stress upon returning to the classroom, and disappointment at missing out on what others were doing.

The students in this book had varied experiences with these special education models. Evette was the only student to spend the majority of her public school years in a self-contained classroom where she was separated from the general education population for the entire school day. When Evette was in fifth grade, her mother, Barbara, pushed for a mainstream placement, as Evette had made little progress in the self-contained classroom.

This mainstream placement, however, had additional problems of which Barbara was not aware when she pushed for this placement: "They feel that mainstreaming allows the kids to be inspired by their [peers]. . . . Instead, it was being put in their faces every single day: 'You're inadequate.' So Evette would feel embarrassed about her work, compared to the other kids'. . . . Instead of it being inspiring, it was actually more disheartening for her." Evette explained that after she had been pulled out to work on something, she fell behind in her regular classwork, so she would be pulled out again. The more she was pulled out, the more she missed in her mainstream classroom: "When you're pulled out, you're missing everything, and then you get pulled out again and again and again to make up for the stuff that you're getting pulled out for."

Polly described her embarrassment whenever the teacher came to the classroom door to take her to the resource room. Polly's mother, Lesley, noted that Polly had difficulty in maintaining friendships as a result of the constant pullout. Lesley questioned the value of the resource room—which, she noted, had the same student-teacher ratio as the regular classroom:

> The regular classroom had twenty students and a teacher and an aide, and the special classroom had one teacher and ten kids, but all with disabilities. She [Polly] would say that she would be working with some girls that she liked, doing a little . . . project in her homeroom, and then get called out. So she didn't have a chance to develop friendships or nice ties with people in *that* environment [general education classroom] because it was always interrupted.

Nancy couldn't pursue her interest in art or get a break from regular schoolwork because her free time was filled up with the resource room. Nancy described her experiences of pullout: "When I would get up, all the kids would look at you, 'oh, they're going somewhere else.' And they knew. 'Cause in seventh grade, my math teacher, he'd call us 'the travelers.'"

In addition to feeling "weird" about going to the resource room, Nancy remembers the difficulty of returning to the classroom and not knowing what the other students were doing: "When I would go back into the class, they would sometimes still be doing math, and they would have things written on the board that I had no idea how to do it. . . . I just felt that I wasn't learning . . . what the other kids were. . . . I was, like, behind."

Nancy recalled that when she was younger she had found it easier to be pulled out, but as she got into later elementary and middle school, she felt embarrassed and behind the other students. Furthermore, she did not feel that the resource room teachers were helping her learn.

Nancy choked back her tears as she described how after finishing a test in the classroom, the test was then put in the resource room where the resource room teachers would erase her answers and tell her to try again. She explained that she was given word boxes to help her find the correct word to put on her paper or just told to keep trying. "I was . . . really, really frustrated, 'cause I thought they would [change my answers]. I want my own answers, not theirs. . . . And I didn't feel like I was learning."

Mike described feeling anxious upon returning to the classroom after being pulled out. He was confused about what he had missed and about not knowing the current classroom work and missing classes he enjoyed. He stated, "I really never knew when, each time I was taken out, a new test was coming or a new book report was coming out. Social studies, I was doing really good at, but I was always out, 'cause I . . . had a teacher who took me out of class during important subjects."

While pullout heightened Mike's anxiety, Frank felt that his identity was defined by being pulled out. Frank's mother, Ella, related what Frank told her:

> It was four times a week, forty-five minutes a day, he was being pulled out, and he hated it. Hated it. He says, "Ma, I'm stupid, huh? Is that why they pull me out?" His anxiety didn't start till, like, second grade, when all this was going on. That's when his anxiety kicked in.

Over time, the parents of all of these students observed flaws in the public schools' special education programs that contributed to their child's struggle with learning to read. Many parents praised some classroom teachers and special education teachers, noting their hard work and good intentions. However, the parents came to realize that despite good intentions, the teachers in this system were simply unable to teach their child.

Mike explained that he did not blame the teachers for not knowing how to teach him: "I had some really nice teachers, I had some really . . . not-so-good teachers; they were all nice, but they didn't really teach the way that I needed to be [taught]." Ella, Frank's mother, also praised the efforts of the teachers, realizing their intentions were good: "They tried to help. I can't say a bad word about the public school system. I have to say they did try to help Frank as much as they could."

Shaywitz's (2003) research reports instances of parents feeling similarly—that teachers were well intentioned but simply untrained and lacking knowledge in "state-of-the-art, evidence-based instructional strategies" (p. 35). Andreasen (2012) noted that some teachers were clearly helpful but many were not. While the approaches of inclusion, mainstreaming, and pullout were designed to help meet the needs of the special education student in the least restrictive environment, for these nine students these models created more hardship that prevented learning rather than enhanced it.

BLAME THE VICTIM

Most of the students in this book experienced blame for their inability to learn to read—from professionals and sometimes also from their parents. The blame may reflect an educational gap in school professionals' and parents' understanding of dyslexia rather than anything intentional. Olson (2009) explains that those without proper training in educational differences often view the child as the problem.

Wolf (2007) notes that children arrive at school full of enthusiasm and energy for learning. As a child with dyslexia advances in school and as reading becomes problematic, the child gets messages of blame from both teachers and parents: "He's told by his parents to try harder; he's told by his teachers that he's 'not working to potential'; he's told by other children that he's a 'retard' and a 'moron'; he gets a resounding message that he's not going to amount to much" (p. 166). Andreasen (2012) reported a child with dyslexia who was misdiagnosed with ADHD and then described as lazy for incomplete work.

The phrase "not working to potential" commonly appeared on the report cards of the students in this story, along with comments such as "defiant" or "lacks effort and focus." Both Evette and Frank admitted they had given up in school, which may account for these negative comments. However, they explained that they had given up only after years of frustration as they struggled to learn to read.

Many of the students reported working hard in school with little result. In time, they gave up trying, and their parents stepped in, doing the child's homework and intervening with teachers in an effort to contain their child's frustration level.

Evette explained that the homework was just too hard. She could not do it, so she stopped trying. Then, because she had stopped doing homework, she lost certain privileges: "If you don't do your homework, you can't go outside; if you don't do your homework, you can't eat a snack. I lost all my privileges. They were taken away, but it's like I slave over some pieces of homework for four hours, just to go outside."

For Evette, losing privileges was not a motivator. She preferred to lose her recess time over trying to do her homework, which she found too difficult. During the last six weeks of fifth grade, the teacher said that Evette had to read for thirty minutes every night in order to participate in special fifth-grade activities. Although Evette desperately wanted to participate in these activities, reading for thirty minutes a night overwhelmed her, and the consequence—being excluded from the special activities—angered her rather than motivated her.

Evette's mother wrote a note indicating the level of her daughter's stress, but the teacher insisted that Evette was just being lazy. In the end, Evette lied about her reading time in order to participate in the fifth-grade activities.

The comments on Evette's IEP and on her report cards indicated that her academic issues were related to emotional problems and that she had the ability to do better academically. For example, one IEP report stated, "Evette's teacher reports that Evette appears to be a child who is carrying a lot inside and often uses academic time to talk about personal issues. Evette's teacher and the school nurse report concerns about Evette's social and emotional functioning."

In addition, the IEP noted, "Evette has developed some learned helplessness around academic tasks that are challenging for her." Evette admitted to giving up on some of her work, but she noted that this came only after years of humiliation and frustration in struggling with assignments that were over her head.

Like the professionals in the school system, Evette's mother, Barbara, pushed her daughter to work hard. Barbara agreed with the teacher that Evette needed the push. In an e-mail to Evette's teacher, Barbara explained that she had tried to push her daughter to work to her potential:

> I am okay that it [a homework assignment] counted as a missed homework because I have been pushing her to do more each day. Her comments have been that everyone is tougher on her since the parent-teacher meeting. I explained to her that we are just trying to get her to work to her potential. Now I get the 'I hate school,' 'I hate reading,' and the occasional 'I hate you, Mom' for pushing her.

Evette's mother, like the professionals, blamed Evette's poor work ethic rather than her disability.

Frank's public school report cards identified a lack of focus and effort as the problem at the heart of Frank's academic struggles. In second grade, Frank's teacher wrote, "Frank enjoys his peers and likes the social part of school. A goal is to become excited about learning."

In third grade, Frank's distractibility was noted. Frank's teacher wrote, "Frank requires consistent redirection and monitoring." The IEP developed that year identified Frank's lack of effort: "Frank's difficulty attending and maintaining focus further interfered with applying himself in the classroom. At times, Frank does not put forth any effort to the task at hand and does nothing."

One of Frank's goals on this IEP related to attention. It stated,

Frank continues to require adult cueing for attention to instruction and to assigned tasks. He does not seem to be motivated to attend or to complete assignments. Sometimes he whines and says, "I don't want to." His attention is characterized by staring off, playing with an object or his pencil, talking to others, looking in his desk or wandering around the room. Discussions and minor consequences have not produced any change.

The consistent message in Frank's reports was that he maintained some choice in the way he approached his schooling. He was blamed for needing adult cuing and for his lack of motivation and focus. But from Frank's perspective, his teachers did little to help him learn to read: "The teacher never asked me to do anything, just sit there all the time and do nothing." Frank also commented, "The homework was pretty easy, but I felt like I wasn't learning anything. . . . I was just talking to friends and never really did anything." In general, Frank's teachers thought that he could be more motivated and focused, and Frank felt that they did little to help him learn.

As with Evette, Raya's problems with learning were blamed on emotional and behavioral difficulties. On Raya's report card from public school, teachers stated that Raya's behavior and emotional problems were getting in the way of her learning. Ms. Kames wrote, "Often she will become defiant and or make excuses for why she is unable to complete an assignment or join the class for a learning experience."

Ms. Rolst, the first-grade teacher, wrote, "Raya's emotions and behavior often affect her reading ability and effort level. It can be difficult to decipher when Raya is having a hard time reading and when she is pretending to be stuck and struggling. She works well when she can have the individual attention of an adult." This series of comments seemed to imply that Raya sought adult attention and that when she got her behavior under control, she might have greater success in her studies. A school psychologist's report likewise suggested that Raya's parents contact a psychologist to address Raya's emotional issues.

Raya reported that both teachers and students blamed her for her disability. She stated that teachers got frustrated when she could not answer a question. As Raya explained, most of the time, she did not understand the class discussions. Therefore, when called on, she simply repeated what she heard other students say. Raya noted she could not add anything new to the discussion because she did not understand.

Raya recalled that other students also blamed her because her work was modified to accommodate her needs: "They'd say, 'It's not fair that you don't do tests and, you don't have to do anything,' because I'm dumb and people would always . . . they'd, like, blame me for things they had to do; like, if they had to write . . . ten sentences, on . . . homework, and I had to write three, they would blame me for them having to do hard work." Thus, modifications in homework that were intended to help Raya cope with the workload and to minimize academic stress created a different type of stress when her peers blamed her for having easier assignments.

James's parents also blamed their child until they fully understood James's learning issues. They described how they tried to get James to keep up with the work during the school day by having the teacher send home the unfinished work. On the weekends during second grade, James would typically work all day on Saturday doing eighteen sheets of homework to stay caught up to the class. James's mother explained, "And . . . we would feel like, OK, well, you know, get the work done! Get the work done!"

While James's parents tried to help him keep up with the work, upon meeting after meeting with his second-grade teacher, they also felt that the teachers were blaming him for not being able to learn. James's mother explained that in multiple IEP meetings, his teachers commented that they were providing him services to match his learning needs, but he was not applying himself.

"And it really started to feel very early on like it was *his* job to fix things, and I think at first, for that second grade, we were like, 'All right, well, you know, we got to work on *him*.' And I think we all put a lot of onus on him to be responsible for fixing whatever the problem was." The school remedy had James staying in for recess to finish homework and isolating him in an individualized cubicle in the back of the classroom. But James continued to struggle. His parents soon realized that trying to get James to work harder was not going to get him to learn.

James stated that he had to stay in for recess "at least twice a week" and that teachers often told him he was not trying hard enough: "It's like, Yes, I'm trying hard enough. If I wasn't trying hard enough, do you think I'd be in tears, every day I came home, because the work was so hard? . . . My fourth grade teacher . . . didn't think that I was trying hard enough; that was the reason why I was lagging behind, so I'm like, I don't get this!" "You're just not trying."

Next day, "This doesn't make any sense."

"Well, try harder."

"I don't understand this."

"You're just not trying hard enough."

James noted that he was prescribed Ritalin for attention deficit disorder (ADD) and took it for two years, but, he said, it only made his anger and emotions worse. His parents acknowledged that they had tried medications for ADD because James's teachers insisted that his focus issues interfered with his learning how to read. When medication did not help him learn to read, his parents explained, his teachers said he was "willful and lazy."

In one meeting with his teacher, James's parents reported that the teacher tried to start with some positive statements but quickly got into negative descriptions: "James is wonderful. James is disorganized. James distracts the class . . . and there'd be this . . . litany of things that he did." As things grew worse, James's parents became worried about larger risks, such as suicide or drug or alcohol addiction, if James were to continue in this environment of blame. At multiple levels, James was being blamed for his learning issues and was being expected to find ways to remediate himself.

Debbie's oldest son, Robert experienced blame when he was accused of faking his disability in order to get attention. Debbie described one meeting with a special education director: "[The] special ed. director [sat] across from him and said, 'You're faking your disability.' I'll never forget that: shaking her finger and saying that to him, and [I'm] saying, 'Oh, sixteen-year-olds always do that. They always fake their disability so they get more attention.' . . . I'm like, come on!"

Debbie also recalled hearing similar statements about her other children, Cally and Tim. She explained, "He doesn't apply himself and he needs to try harder. . . . I did hear that a lot. 'Well, you know, he's a boy, he doesn't write neat—he needs to try harder.' I heard the same thing about Tim."

Mike recalled that teachers blamed him when they got frustrated with him for not working fast enough. He remembered one teacher "telling me I need to work faster; . . . 'You don't have all day.' They would take me out in private and, like, 'Can you maybe work, 'cause I don't want to wait at least twenty minutes for you to work on one problem.' Like, 'OK, I'm sorry.'" Mike felt bad about his speed but also knew he was doing the best he could.

Mike recalled that a gym teacher once blamed him for not understanding directions and then called him a name. "He [the gym teacher] screamed at people when you're not getting in the right position. For instance, if I'm standing on the sideline, he wants me to stand on the other one, 'cause . . . the way he talks I can't really interpret it right. 'No, not over there, you idiot, over there.'"

Blame for these students took the form of requests to work faster, harder, with more interest, more focus, and more accuracy. Some of the students had teachers who felt that emotional issues were blocking their learning potential. Yet these students were not alone in feeling blamed for their disability.

Shaywitz (2003) reported that in the early 1900s, the eye surgeon E. Treacher Collins, who studied "word blindness" (the term then used for dyslexia), observed students who were blamed and bullied for a learning disability they had inherited through no fault of their own. Schwarz (2006) acknowledges that the blame-the-victim mentality remains an issue—one that is left over from the 1950s model of special education. Olson (2009) also noted that students with learning disabilities often felt "unfairly blamed" (p. 104) for their lack of effort, behavioral issues, and defiance, when in fact it was their learning disabilities that were interfering with their ability to learn. Ates, Rasinski, Yildirim, and Yildiz (2012) reported students in Turkey with diagnosis of dyslexia also experienced blame from both their parents and their teachers.

For the students Olson studied, blame often led to self-blame, which resulted in depression—a common diagnosis for these nine students as well. Olson describes how students in her study maintained this sense of self-blame throughout their years of schooling, thinking of themselves as stupid and incapable of learning despite their tremendous effort to perform.

Blame often appears in times of frustration, when students, teachers, and parents cannot make sense of a child's inability to learn and when all remedies seem to have been exhausted. Schwarz (2006) explains that because of the self-contained special education classrooms implemented in response to the 1975 Individuals with Disabilities Education Act (IDEA), many general education teachers today are left unprepared to deal with a diverse range of learners who are mainstreamed into their classrooms. Additionally, Salend (2016) suggests that some educators feel they have inadequate training and support to work with some children with disabilities. There are no winners in the blame game. Students suffer emotional consequences, adults' concerns are never addressed, and the student's disability needs are not met.

EMOTIONAL AND FINANCIAL SACRIFICES

The students and families in this book experienced many sacrifices in their journey to the Kelsey School. Some parents paid for private tutoring and private testing, while all the parents paid for lawyer and advocate fees. They spent countless hours working with school personnel to get services to help their child learn, and then they spent innumerable hours fighting with the same people to get their child an out-of-district placement.

For some students and parents, the emotional strain of this arduous journey had lasting effects. One child cried whenever she retold her story from her public school days, and her mother developed an illness that doctors determined was likely brought on by stress. Other parents felt their child's self-esteem plummeted during these troublesome years of schooling. As tireless advocates demanding services, parents also dealt with negative perceptions of themselves from school professionals.

Some families, understanding the financial and emotional commitment required to get their child to Kelsey, recognized the inequity of a system that relies on parental resources and supports. The parents of the students in this book all received some funding from their district schools for their child's education at Kelsey, a private school for students with learning disabilities. Funding amounts varied depending on what each town offered, the nature of the child's disability, and the nature of their legal battle. Some were fully funded by their towns, while the majority received partial funding.

Barbara borrowed money from her mother for Evette's first year while she brought a lawsuit against the town for inadequacies in educating her child. The agreements between families and school systems varied between districts and between individual families. Multiple factors such as where a child lives, the nature of the child's disability, and the lawyer hired can determine how much money a family ultimately will have to pay. When the law stipulates that all children are entitled to an education, it seems odd that individual families need to advocate for their children and demand services while paying lawyers to negotiate a desirable outcome.

Mary hired a lawyer when no one from the school system contacted her after she had submitted the outside testing performed on her daughter. The lawyer walked Mary through the steps of applying to Kelsey and another school. With her lawyer's representation, Mary then began the fight to persuade the school system to pay for both summer school and the regular school year at Kelsey. Mary, a single mother, lacked the $50,000 she needed for legal fees and her daughter Beth's tuition at Kelsey, but she knew she needed to make it work:

> I was panic stricken over the money. I'm like, "I don't have this kind of money. Where am I going to come up with this kind of money?" And then . . . I don't know, it was like . . . an epiphany. I was just sitting there and after two days or so, I went, "How can I not do this? So what if I ruin my credit rating? Who cares? How could you leave someone to flounder like that?" It was like she was in a lake and I wasn't doing anything to pull her out. So, I said, "I *have* to do this." So . . . I just got great big student loans. And I said, "You know what? The worst that could happen is . . . and it won't happen, is that I would have to pay the whole thing back."

Mary then began the fight to get the school system to pay. While many families make compromises, Mary was unwilling to settle. She explained,

> After this much time, I wasn't willing to try anything else. I gave them two years of kindergarten and grades one, two, three, four. My child's life was passing her by. Well, they told me how wonderful she was doing in school, what a wonderful child she was, and how she tried so hard and everybody loved her. But nowhere does it say that Beth could read. So . . . I wasn't willing . . . and I told my attorney that: "I'm not willing to play footsie with them anymore. It's . . . she goes to Kelsey and they pay. *That's* the way it is now. They lost their chance."

Mary succeeded in obtaining full funding for her daughter to attend Kelsey. However, she recognized the injustice of a system that only allows some children to receive this privileged education and a system that had put her through so much to get there:

I find it completely reprehensible that there are so many children that need help that will never get it, because they can't borrow sixty, seventy, eighty thousand dollars . . . while they fight with the school department to get the child what the child needs. 'Cause I said that to my lawyer; I go, "What happens to people? People who are from foreign countries . . . people who don't *know* any better?"

She goes, "Their kids end up in jail or on welfare."

I'm like, "It's not right." You know? You shouldn't *have* to do these . . . ridiculous things. And some of the things I had to do are ridiculous . . . just ridiculous.

In addition to the injustice of needing finances to fight for your child's education, Mary noted how people comment about the funds spent on special education:

And then, you have to deal with people who think that you have no right to take the money out. . . . I think . . . what's wrong with people? Every child deserves to learn to read; every child deserves to get the education to the best of their ability, whatever their ability is. And I'm . . . just angry that . . . they put me through so much, they put my child through so much, . . . when it's something that should be . . . every child's right.

Mary further explained how this fight for her child's education consumed her life. She also drew an analogy to her line of work—policing—noting how it might look if the same standards were applied:

So, it was very grueling. It was very, very grueling. It took over my life. People hated to see me coming; I know they did, 'cause I knew that . . . I was at times all consumed by this fight, as opposed to everything else in my life. I kind of resent it, to be honest with you . . . because . . . I wouldn't treat people that way, in my profession, you don't . . . if something happens to you . . . . If you walked out of here now, and somebody hit you with a baseball bat to steal your purse, we would do *everything* to put him in jail . . . *everything* we could. We wouldn't ask you what kind of person you were, how much money you had.

The differential treatment offered to some children with the resources to find their way to Kelsey disturbed Mary. In her career in police work, as she noted, the police act on a person's behalf regardless of their background. Many of the parents in this story understood how both financial and emotional stress disqualified many students from finding their way to Kelsey.

Despite the high cost of sending a child to Kelsey, both in tuition and in legal fees to win the battle with the district school, many of these parents knew they could not allow financial hardships to deter them from sending their child to Kelsey. In a conversation with her husband, Paul, Libby acknowledged the cost of sending her daughter to private school but also noted the absence of another option:

> I don't care if I have to pay for it, Paul. I don't care. She is *not* going back there [the public school system]. I know what Kelsey can do for her for the summer, and I know what this public school is doing, and it's not it. And I did everything the lawyer asked me to do, and . . . from second to sixth grade, excluding the lawyer, has cost us about $40,000, and I have a husband who's on a disability at thirty-five, so I'm the only one working. And I was like, "I don't care if I have to remortgage my house. She is going to Kelsey." And she would write in her diary every day: "I hate school. I hate school. I don't get it. No one understands me. I really want to go to Kelsey."

Libby explained the emotional sacrifices while noting the hardship for those who do not have support:

> And I don't wish that on another child to be tormented. I mean, I thank God that I have my parents, I have four sisters and Paul's parents that . . . financially helped us out, emotionally helped us out, 'cause there were days where I would be like, I don't even want to get out of bed. 'Cause I don't even know what the next . . . task is going to be. It was just so draining.

Libby recounted the cost and sacrifices on their lives both in time and their health:

> We finally get our lives back together [when Nancy started to attend Kelsey], this poor girl doesn't have to go from testing to this, . . . to be pulled out, you know? She's accepted where she is. My husband has two health issues neurologically, so we're at the doctors for him. I found out, ten years ago, I became a Type 1 diabetic, and . . . they think that was stress . . . brought on [by] the years . . . helping Nancy . . . there was no family history of it. I had a lot, that whole year.

In Libby's case, the fight to get Nancy a viable education took its toll in both financial and emotional sacrifices. Libby developed a stress-related illness but continued the fight until she secured Nancy's placement at Kelsey—an environment in which she surmised that Nancy would thrive.

For James's parents, the emotional stress and strain on both the family and the child during their years laboring for the proper education outweighed any of the financial stress and the ultimate fight with the school system to obtain funding. Peter, James's father, explained: "Financial stress is *nothing* compared to the kind of stress of your child failing and looking at this poor other kid who'd committed suicide, and thinking that could be your kid in four years."

Research shows that Peter's response is prescient. Adolescents with reading difficulties have higher rates of suicide than those without reading difficulties, suggesting the life-or-death importance of helping children learn to read (Stephanie, Adam, David, Elizabeth, et al., 2006, Crouch & Pataki, 2016).

Ella mentioned her intent to pay an advocate, whatever the cost, to enlist help at her IEP meetings. Without the advocate, Ella feared that she would not be able to obtain the necessary services for Frank: "I paid her. She goes, 'It will cost . . . ,' [and] I'm like, 'I don't care what it's going to cost me, you come to *every* meeting with me.' And I did, I paid for her to drive to and from the meeting, and I paid for her to come to the meeting. I didn't care what it was going to cost me, I was going to have her there."

Ella became emotional as she recalled the moment she heard that Frank was accepted to Kelsey. She relayed both the joy and then the panic as she thought about finding the means to finance the tuition. Immediately, Ella contacted her advocate, who telephoned the town's special education director. The advocate, aware that the school system would deny funding, instructed Ella to retain a specific lawyer from a well-known Boston firm. Instantly, Ella began incurring more fees:

> So, I called [the lawyers] and they told me to fax everything over: the core evaluations, all my IEP stuff. They said, "And while you're in the process, you need to send us a retainer fee of $15,000." I just choked. So I called my husband up and I'm like, "What do we do now?" and he goes, "Well, we have life insurance we can cash in." So I said, "OK," and we called the life insurance place and they're like, "Yep." If you need the money, you can borrow against it." And we're like, "OK."

The advocate called the school with the name of the lawyer. With this new information, the school acquiesced, and agreed to pay for Kelsey. Despite the additional legal expenses she had incurred, Ella recalled that she felt as though she had won the lottery that day.

Debbie moved so that her children could attend Kelsey. Debbie's family lived on a farm six hours' drive from Kelsey. She rented a small apartment in a neighboring town, leaving behind her husband and farm. She described the strain on her marriage and the difficulty of maintaining her home:

> In the beginning, we went home at least one weekend a month, and, of course, holidays and things like that. But it was . . . very, very hard on my husband. He lost his job within three months that we were away. . . . He was working at a nursing home, [and] now he's driving a bus, [so] that was a big hardship, 'cause we had to pay health coverage for a couple of months, and things like that. Emotionally, it's been very hard for him; he feels like we've deserted him, 'cause he definitely has the same learning disabilities they have. . . . So we all just lived in this one-bedroom apartment, and we have a picture of all these blow-up beds in this one room. . . . It's become a big strain on our marriage.

Debbie noted that the trip home has become harder, leaving the children with less time to see their father. But leaving a home she loved and even jeopardizing her marriage were sacrifices she felt she had to make in order to get her children the education they needed:

> They do miss their life. We did have a nice little happy family life on the farm. They do miss that and they see what it's done with, you know, it's strained now between them and Dad. . . . And it's really put us financially in debt—unbelievable, . . . especially with Cally, this is the third year we're footing the tuition. . . . And . . . no amount of money could ever equate to what it's done for my kids. [*Gets emotional.*] . . . This is one window of opportunity in my kids' lifetime, and I could say, "Well, I'll put that on hold for me. But this . . . I *have* to do this; I can't put this on hold for them." I can't say, . . . [when they're] thirty-five, "Oh, I wish I had done that for them." . . . I know that when they get out of here, they're going to have the normal bumps and bruises, rather than the normal bumps and bruises *along with* baggage. They're not going to have that baggage dragging them down on top of it.

Debbie experienced first-hand how school personnel might deny a child an appropriate education. Her older son graduated from high school with a sixth-grade reading level and continues to struggle. He began receiving help when he started to attend Kelsey's affiliated college. From this experience, Debbie knew the consequences of relying on the public school system to educate her children in the way they needed. Her sacrifices for her children were both emotional and financial, and also life altering.

The parents in this story experienced both financial and emotional sacrifices as they pursued their efforts to have their child attend the Kelsey School. They noted their own suffering while at the same time acknowledging their privilege in having the means to assume the financial burden of pursuing an accessible education and the ability to obtain the necessary support systems to go through the process.

While the public school system presents as providing an equal education for all children, privilege in schooling has been widely challenged both in the division of resources and in the way students gain access to better education (Darling-Hammond, 2004; Gold & Heraldo, 2012; Kozol, 1991; Oakes, 1985; Olson, 2009). The parents of these children with learning disabilities enjoyed the advantage of getting their child to Kelsey, while at the same time understanding how many other children are left behind.

COPING STRATEGIES

Both the students and the parents in this story developed coping strategies to deal with the stress and pain of school. The students reported hating school until they enrolled at Kelsey. Some of the strategies for coping were widely used; others were unique to particular children. For the parents, completing their child's homework was one common strategy for dealing with their frustrations of watching their child struggle. For students, a common strategy was faking sickness as well as other school-avoidance techniques. For example, Evette had seventy-two tardies during her fifth-grade year, which was her last year in public school.

Evette's mother explained her difficulties in getting Evette to school: "I was dragging her to school. I even threatened to drag her in her pajamas. I was literally, physically, dragging her out of bed and pulling her by her hair a few times, . . . just whatever I could do to get her up and out. And by the time we'd get down there, we were anywhere from five to ten to fifteen minutes late."

Evette explained that she would kick, scream, yell, and do whatever else she could to avoid going to school. She tried putting the hairdryer to her forehead to simulate a fever and ripping up her homework, then saying she could not go to school because she had not done her homework. Evette described her school day as "torture." According to her mother, she was well known to the school nurse and occasionally called her mother from her cell phone to say that she was sick.

Other students developed day-to-day strategies. For Raya, it was getting out of the classroom as much as possible. Raya found the school nurse's office a haven from the stress of school: "She started coming home and she had about 200 'I love the nurse' stickers on her folder. It was like [the] *entire* folder was covered with [them], and when she pulled that out I was, like, 'Why do you have so many of those?' She goes, 'Oh, well, I like the nurse.' She'd go . . . to the nurse to get out of class . . . like, 'I'm out of here,' . . . 'My stomach hurts,' that kind of thing."

Raya used other coping strategies as well. She copied from students she perceived as smarter and answered questions randomly on standardized tests. In the classroom, Raya explained, she would listen to what the "smart" kids were saying: "I would listen to what they said because most of them are smarter than me, and then I would say the same thing because I didn't know what to say." Raya's mother explained further that when Raya was unable to finish her work, she had to put it in a green box to work on later. Raya found it embarrassing to put work in the green box, so she copied from others. In addition, she asked friends to tell her about books they were reading so she could talk about the book:

> The teacher would ask questions, and she would raise her hand, stand up, and . . . it appears as if she was reading the book, and I told her teacher that, she was like, "Well, you know . . . she's very interactive in class, and . . ." And I said, "She's not . . . she can't read that book, her friend's telling her everything about it." And then she used to have her sister read to her at home, and

then she used to put a bookmark in the book and then verbalize what she had read, but she . . . was faking.

Raya's mother described Raya as a "professional at hiding her disability." On standardized tests, when Raya had to fill in bubbles to answer questions, she just filled them in randomly:

> There was a sentence and you had to answer it, like, A, B, C, and D. And I couldn't read it, and I didn't know the answer, and I just . . . filled in each bubble . . . 'cause I was like, "Oh yeah, this is going to take me forever," and I was so scared 'cause everybody was, like, on the third page when I was on the first problem. . . . And so I just bubble-filled, and I was actually the first one done, and everybody was like, "Oh, my God! Raya, you are so smart," I was, like, "Yeah."

Raya used multiple strategies to get her through her day. She used visits to the school nurse as a way to stay out of the classroom. She used her friends to camouflage her disability. Raya appeared successful, as she was never put on an IEP.

James, like Raya, relied on friends to help him with his work. Rather than use the school nurse, he told "outlandish" stories to explain his missing work. His parents explained:

> So . . . as school broke down, this wonderful, rich, vivid imagination became sort of his comfort zone. . . . [He told stories] to mask the fact that school was hard. . . . I think it was, "Gee, you know, James, you didn't do your work." "I'm sorry, I'm really tired." "Well, why are you tired?" "My father dragged me outside in the middle of the night." You know, [he would say that his dad] woke him up at two in the morning to go outside with night vision goggles, and they were out in the woods.

Mike developed his own unique coping strategy: He learned to be an outstanding chess player. "I beat a lot of people, and people who called me stupid, I played them in chess and beat them, and they didn't really say anything to me anymore. So . . . it was pretty much my way of saying, 'Don't call me stupid ever again.'" Evelyn, Mike's mother, added that Mike would actually make sure he had a good crowd and then he would "cream" the other player. It was Mike's way of getting back at kids that embarrassed him about his academic challenges.

Similar to Evette, Mike faked being sick to avoid school. When he told his mother he was sick but had no fever, she would say he had to stay in bed all day. He did this without objection, preferring to stay in bed all day with the curtains drawn than to go to school. Evelyn felt sure she had solved the problem of his feigning sickness by making him stay in bed all day, but she soon realized that she needed to adjust her policy to a "no fever, no staying home" rule.

Frank also faked illness to get out of school. Ella explained that Frank would call her from school on a regular basis: "I mean, *every* day, to get Frank to public school, *every* day was . . . 'I have a stomachache, I don't feel good, I got to throw up.' Every single morning was like that. He'd call me from school, 'I don't feel good. Can you come get me?' It was *always* like that."

Nancy sobbed when recalling her years before coming to Kelsey. She explained, "Sometimes . . . I would skip school because I just couldn't deal with it. . . . Like, I would skip a Friday and then I'd have the weekend to, like, recover, and then I'd have to go back Monday morning."

For these students, school represented a place of shame, embarrassment, and difficulty that required creative thinking to avoid. So they feigned illness, excused themselves to the nurse, called parents from school, and found alternative ways to maintain a sense of their own intelligence. In these ways, they managed to survive in an environment that challenged their sense of confidence rather than supported them.

PARENT COPING STRATEGIES

The parents in this story strongly identified with their children as a way of coping with the stress and struggles the children were enduring. This was evident in parents' use of the pronoun "we" and in their involvement in their child's homework. The education of their child became a family project requiring hours of work by the parent, mostly the mother, doing or supporting the child's work in keeping up with school assignments.

The parents often used the pronoun "we" rather than the child's name when they spoke of their child's work. For example, Mel, Raya's mother, described the process of teaching Raya her letters: "*We* definitely had a hard time remembering letters." Libby, Nancy's mother, also used "we" when she talked about Nancy's grades: "*We*'re getting C-pluses, a couple of B's, and she's . . . you know . . . 'Needs to participate more in class.' She comes in with her homework and . . . it was because *we* did it."

Libby, knowing that Nancy struggled with homework, often did it for her—a common strategy for the families. Many parents started by helping their child with homework and, in many cases, moved to just doing the homework for their child to avoid witnessing their child's frustration. When Mary, Beth's mother, went to talk with the teacher about the homework, she used the pronoun "we," as homework truly was a group effort. Mary explained:

We would sit and do it together for hours. She'd be in the third grade, we'd be doing two, three hours of homework a night. And I went to them and I said, "*We can't* do this. This is horrifying; *we* can't do this." "Oh, well, just do the best you can. Oh, and we'll make some modifications." So they made modifications, like if they had a paper with ten math problems on it, she only had to do three.

Mary described the modifications as unhelpful, however, because Beth could not read the directions. So Mary read the directions, leaving Beth dependent on her mother to complete her homework assignments.

Evette's mother, Barbara, also pushed for homework modifications. However, in some cases, the modifications were insufficient to allow Evette to work independently. Despite Barbara's insistence that the work overwhelmed Evette, the teacher refused to modify further. At this point, Barbara started doing the homework for Evette, knowing that it was above her daughter's ability:

I'd be doing the reading with her because she couldn't access that material because it was difficult for her to read. I would read it, I'd have to explain it, and I felt that I was doing more of the teaching, which is why we would butt heads on occasion in fifth grade. There would be times that, because she would be so frustrated doing it, I'd say, "OK." And I would put down, "Dictated by Evette," because that was part of her IEP, that I could scribe for her. And, you know, it got to be the point that I scribed a lot.

Barbara scribed more than she wanted and, at other times, found herself actually doing Evette's homework. She related the unbearable struggles that ensued as she tried to get Evette to do her homework. Barbara explained, "What we'd end up doing, is end up in a screaming match sometimes because she just wouldn't want to get it done, and I'd end up finishing it off so that it would just be done."

Mike noted that he was unable to do the homework by himself: "I think about 95 percent of the time, Mom had to help me do my homework. She pretty much had to do the note cards. She had to tell me the answers. She had to write everything down in a big textbook."

Mike's mother, Evelyn, reported that she was working twenty hours a week helping Mike with his homework. She ordered books on tape for him, organized his spelling words, and gave him study sheets for tests. She felt this consumed the whole family, affecting vacation time as well: "It was like this big noose around our neck, constantly, constantly. Vacation time—wait! What vacation? We're spending it catching up and doing these horrible projects!" Evelyn knew she needed to help Mike in order for him to progress and to avoid embarrassment at school. For both Evelyn and Mike, Mike's schoolwork became all consuming.

Frank's mother, Ella, explained that she got tired of arguing with Frank about homework and, eventually, just did the work for him, because she knew he was not able to do it independently:

> The frustration was horrid; to sit there and argue with him. . . . I was arguing with a kid that could not do it, 'cause he didn't have the *tools* to do it. He didn't *know* how to do it. To even write a sentence. And you know, towards the end, I would just, "Here. Gimme. I'll write this." And I'd write the sentences down for him and I'd give him, "Here, copy it." 'Cause I just couldn't deal with it anymore.

Tim was having shutdowns in school and the parents found themselves doing the homework just to get him to school: "He was just having a hard time and he [was] having shutdowns in the classroom and homework, at home a lot of times, he refused to do it, and basically, my husband and I did it. It was the worst thing you could do for your kid, and I think every special ed. parent makes that mistake in the beginning: You think you're helping them, and you're not."

These students developed their own coping mechanism to get through a difficult and stressful day of struggling to compete at the academic level of their peers. Their parents also reached heightened levels of frustration, sometimes finding it easier to do the child's homework rather than engaging in a nightly battle. The child's educational experience intruded into family life, as noted by one parent who felt the family could not vacation and by other parents who used the pronoun "we" in describing their child's work. The all-encompassing nature of trying to help a child learn without the necessary tools and support pushed these parents to find another way.

The nine students in this book entered kindergarten ready to learn, but found instead a set of circumstances that created barriers to their education. They were expected to conform to a model of teaching that required them to come and go from the classroom, they had to deal with the blame placed upon them for their disability, they experience emotional stress and their families endure financial hardships. These unexpected consequences of schooling required the students and their parents to find coping strategies that ultimately detracted from the learning process.

While these children suffered, they were the lucky ones who, through their parents' ardent advocacy, found their way to a private school where they were able to get an education that catered to their learning needs. Not all children have these option. In fact, most do not.

Chapter Two

Special Education

How Did We Get Here?

From its inception, special education was designed to separate students who did not fit a socially constructed norm. The educational barriers created by this separation persist today despite attempts to address this issue through legislation such as the least-restrictive-environment provision in the Individuals with Disabilities Education Act (IDEA).

The model of special education has been described as a deficit model and a medical model (Baglieri et al., 2011; Crawford & Bartolome, 2010; Gold & Heraldo, 2012). In such a model, special-education students are labeled (for example, "learning disabled" or "cognitively impaired") on the basis of a deficit or deficiency that needs fixing. At the heart of this model is the belief that student failure results from a deficiency within the student rather than from systemic factors.

It is unclear whether the social construct of special education helps or hinders the students it is designed to benefit. Many believe that this system leads to the creation of arbitrary criteria that serve largely to advance the dominant culture while also promoting racism, sexism, and classism (Baglieri et al., 2011; Crawford & Bartolome, 2010; Dudley-Marling & Gurn, 2010; Ferri, 2010; Gold & Heraldo, 2012; Hart-Tervalon & Garcia, 2014; Herzik, 2015; Willis, 2010). Students who are caught within the confines of this labeling system are often over- or underdiagnosed, sometimes with lifelong consequences (Gold & Heraldo, 2012; Harry & Klingner, 2014; Herzik, 2015; Shaywitz, 2003). The social construction of the dyslexia label provides an example of the dangers associated with this deficit model of diagnosis.

THE EVOLUTION OF SPECIAL EDUCATION

In the context of public schooling, the construct of *special education* has evolved over the years. Its roots are deeply embedded in the political and societal influences that have shaped the way students are educated (Crawford & Bartolome, 2010; Herzik, 2015). In the early twentieth century, as newly written education laws required all children within a specified age range to attend school, students with disabilities moved from their home environments or other private care facilities into segregated spaces in public schools. This was the beginning of the process of separating special education students from the general or "normal" population.

This separation did not necessarily provide special education students with the kind of education they needed, but it did separate them from the general population while also labeling them as "other." With the development of IQ or intelligence quotient testing, the number of students identified as needing special education grew, and testing provided "proof" of differing abilities that solidified the concept of special education. This sorting of students on the basis of standardized testing has served to maintain social stratification rather than actually educating labeled children to an equal standard (Gold & Heraldo, 2012; Harry & Klingner, 2014).

Major changes to the construct of special education developed during the era of the Civil Rights Movement, particularly after the historic 1954 *Brown v. Board of Education* Supreme Court decision. Disabilities rights activists began demanding equal education for children with disabilities on the basis that an equal education could not be separate, as defined by the *Brown* decision. The result was the passage of two pieces of legislation designed to promote the rights of disabled students—the Rehabilitation Act of 1973 and the Education for All Handicapped Children Act of 1975 (P.L. 94-142) (Salend, 2016).

These laws were precursors of the current Individuals with Disabilities Education Act (IDEA), passed in 1990 and most recently reauthorized in 2004. Each reauthorization of IDEA brought many changes, including new categories of disabilities and increased access to due process if a disabled child was not receiving appropriate services. Even with all these legislative changes, however, students who struggled in the general education classroom continued to be categorized and labeled as having a deficit that separated them from the perceived norm (Baglieri et al., 2011; Herzik, 2015).

Within the construct of special education, IDEA is designed to ensure that students obtain "a free and appropriate education" in the "least restrictive environment" available (Crawford & Bartolome, 2010, p. 157; Wright & Wright, 2015). The term "least restrictive environment" has been used to promote the creation of an inclusive environment for special education students in which they would no longer be separated from their general education peers (Rozalski, Stewart, & Miller, 2010; Salend, 2016). However, the term remains difficult to define and may be interpreted differently depending on the school system and the student.

Placement of special education students is determined individually by each student's school-based educational team. Parents have a legal right to challenge any placement made by the team. The standard of least restrictive environment assumes that the best educational environment for children receiving special-education services is with their general education peers.

Nugent (2008) and Fuchs et al. (2015) question the broad assumptions of inclusion, suggesting that two students with similar learning profiles may differ in the benefit they receive from an inclusive placement versus a separate "special education." Nugent notes that the special-education discourse on inclusion fails to incorporate qualitative data examining the perspectives of both students and parents on the best learning environment.

On the basis of interviews with students and parents, conducted as part of her research on Irish students with dyslexia, Nugent (2008) found that students in separate special education schools were "happier" (p. 203) than students with similar profiles placed in more inclusive settings. Nugent acknowledges the political ramifications of "segregated" schooling and how this influences school placement. As she notes, "The word 'segregated' has implications relating to racism, inequality and social rejection" (p. 202).

But although she acknowledges that a child who attends a "special school" may be stigmatized, in fact her research has demonstrated the opposite effect. Students in her study felt more stigmatized by having to read in front of their general education peers and by leaving the classroom to receive special services than they did attending a school for special education students. In addition, she notes that students with severe dyslexia felt more comfortable surrounded by similar peers.

According to Nugent, children with dyslexia who are placed with similar peers compare themselves to those peers and, as a result, develop a better self-concept then those placed in general education environments, where they compare themselves to peers who do not have dyslexia. Noting the positive social experiences of children placed in a school with similar peers, Nugent questions the lack of attention given to social experience when making decisions based solely on the concept of "least restrictive environment."

Fuchs et al.'s (2015) research suggests that placing students with disabilities in classes with nondisabled peers does not ensure access to an appropriate education and may deny the students with disabilities the direct instruction they need to address a skill deficit. Furthermore, it is well documented that learning environments in schools vary, as do diagnoses of learning disabilities. The criteria for a student needing special education in one school system may not be the same in another school system.

Whether inclusion or separation is the goal, the construct of "special education" necessitates some process for sorting children—a process that, in itself, defines some children as "normal" and others as "special"—or, by implication, "abnormal" (Baglieri et al., 2011; Gurn, 2010). This labeling process has significant consequences for those who receive the abnormal label, as well as for those who do not quite fit the criteria and, as a result, are denied services they need.

The sorting process in special education is based on statistical analysis, which compares individual students to an average, represented by a bell-shaped curve with the "average" at its highest point. However, the idea that human intelligence can be normed is itself a social construct, with significant consequences for those who fall at the bottom of the curve. As Gurn (2010) explains, only random events distribute along a normal curve, and human intelligence, although it varies between individuals, is not random.

According to Ball and Harry (2010), trying to establish a norm makes no sense given the many factors that make up each person's individuality, including race, socioeconomic status, immigration status, geographic location, gender, and language. Ball and Harry suggest that inequities are inherent in creating such a norm, which standardizes average or "normal" achievement for students on the basis of the White, middle-class majority. This population, they argue, becomes the standard by which the norm is measured.

Crawford and Bartolome (2010) note that although the normed group is never actually defined, "It is clear that it [the normal group] is made up of White, middle-class, native English-speaking, and able-bodied students who, by virtue of their class standing, possess the type of cultural capital expected in school" (p. 152).

Willis (2010) explains that the social construction of "normal" limits the access and opportunities available to non-dominant groups. Baglieri et al. (2011) contend that despite the claim by the inclusion movement that students are no longer segregated into special-education classes, a division still exists between students who are simply referred to as "kids" and other students who are labeled as "inclusive kids" (p. 14).

The use of the normal curve in education suggests that some students must fail, despite the stated goal of the Every Student Succeeds Act of 2015 (the successor to the No Child Left Behind Act of 2002) that all students must be successful. Despite the many issues inherent in relating the normal curve to education, this measure remains central to the special-education sorting process. Special education continues to rely on a deficit model, whereby students must be labeled with a deficiency as a prerequisite for gaining access to the education they need (Baglieri et al., 2011; Gelb, 2010).

CONSEQUENCES OF THE DEFICIT MODEL

Numerous problems arise for students trapped within the confines of this deficit model of special education. For the purposes of this book, four consequences are most relevant:

1. The child, rather than the education system, is blamed for the deficit.
2. Separate curricula with different expectations are provided for different groups of students.
3. The learning disability label has a negative impact on the emotional life of labeled children and their families.
4. The political and social pressures that influence the special education sorting process perpetuate racism, classism, and sexism and reinforce inequities in social capital.

Blaming the Child, Not the System

When a child is identified as having a learning disability, the child "owns" the problem of not learning at the pace set by the "normal" children in the classroom. In this way, the child is blamed for not learning and is perceived as having a deficit rather than being affected by factors outside of his or her control, such as a mismatch between the instruction offered and the child's learning need (Ball & Harry, 2010; Sailor, 2015).

Children should not have to be labeled in order to receive the education they need. Rogers and Mancini (2010) describe a similar problem with the deficit model with respect to students labeled with ADHD (attention-deficit/hyperactivity disorder). These children discover that in order to be successful, they must take medication. In this way, the disorder becomes the child's problem, which the child must fix with medication.

Harry and Klingner (2014) note that in their research, many students were identified with a learning disability when, in fact, "school practices, such as limited opportunity to learn, present a powerful explanation for many children's educational outcomes" (p. 68), rather than any deficit within the child. Hart-Tervalon and Garcia (2014) add that often it is the teacher's lack of instructional knowledge, including cultural competency, rather than a deficit on the part of the child that leads to the special-education referral.

Olson (2009) notes that teachers often tell special-education students that "if they would just try harder they would do better in school" (p. 103). Yet, in her interviews, Olson found that students wanted to do well and worked hard but felt they were unable to succeed. The result of this unfair blame, Olson noted, was often defiant behavior, which led to further exclusion and a reduction in opportunities to learn. In fact, special education students are disproportionately disciplined in schools, resulting in higher suspension rates—highest for Black males with disabilities (Losen et al., 2015).

Different Curricula for Different Students

A second problem for students who are separated from the general population through their special education identification is the implicit permission to provide one curriculum, and perhaps one teaching methodology, to the general population while establishing different curricula and lower expectations for those not in the general population.

Dudley-Marling and Gurn (2010) note the dangers of assuming that most students are clustered around the average. This allows teachers to use a "one size fits all" (p. 19) curriculum and promotes the expectation that all students will learn through a single methodology, ignoring natural differences in student learning. Again, this approach has the potential for identifying the struggling student as the problem.

Robust research suggests that students who are removed from the general population receive undifferentiated instruction, poorly trained teachers, and lowered expectations, thereby ensuring a lower quality of instruction for students who are removed from the general education classroom (Ball & Harry, 2010; Crawford & Bartolome, 2010; Harry & Klingner, 2014; Maccartney, 2010; Salend, 2016).

The Consequences of Labeling

A third problem with the segregation of some students defined with the special-education label is the effect of this labeling on students' feelings about themselves as learners (Maccartney, 2010; Gold & Richards, 2012). When special education students compare themselves to the normed group, this lowers their sense of their own ability or self-efficacy (Gurn, 2010). Gurn (2010) and Baglieri et al. (2011) suggest that labeling affects special education students' status. Students identified as "disabled" are seen as "problematic and in need of fixing" (p. 242).

Olson (2009) comments that labels assigned to children tend to become "self-perpetuating and self-confirming" (p. 48). Students begin to view themselves as less able than the normed population simply because of the treatment they receive as a result of the "disabled" label—being pulled out of class for extra help or even being identified as lazy by teachers (Olson, 2009). Currently, the special-education label is necessary to get services, but in fact, all students should be able to get the education they need without first receiving this potentially damaging label (Gelb, 2010; Gold & Richards, 2012).

The fact that the social construct of special education involves a sorting system for children implies that an accurate system exists for placing each child in the appropriate learning environment. In fact, the sorting process is far from perfect.

Both Shaywitz (2003) and Harry and Klingner (2014) report inconsistencies in the referral and diagnosis process from teacher to teacher, school to school, and state to state. Shaywitz notes that in her research on 445 students in Connecticut schools, "less than one-third of the children who were reading below their age, ability, or grade level were receiving school services for their reading difficulty" (p. 30).

Furthermore, she found that boys were three to four times as likely as girls to be identified with dyslexia, although in her study of this same population of Connecticut students, she found equal numbers of boys and girls with dyslexia. Identification of dyslexia, then, often depends on what the classroom teacher sees and therefore greatly varies from classroom to classroom and school to school (Shaywitz, 2003).

Harry and Klingner (2014) contend that criteria for special-education referrals are not only random but often overtly racist, leading to overrepresentation of minority children in special education. Crawford and Bartolome (2010) suggest that this overrepresentation of minority students dates back to the desegregation of schools after the 1954 *Brown* decision, when placing minority students in special education was a way of circumventing court-ordered desegregation. As documented by Harry and Klingner (2014) and Herzik (2015), this trend continues today.

Political and Social Pressures

The fourth consequence of the deficit special education model is seen in the many ways in which the sorting process reflects political and social pressures rather than a scientific measure of a child's abilities. For example, Harry and Klingner (2014) note that referral to special education may depend on a school's need to have its students attain high test scores. In this situation, students may be referred to special education simply to remove them from the general education pool, not because of specific problems with their academic performance.

As Harry and Klingner suggest, "The overrepresentation of minority groups in special education should not be understood to mean that these children 'have' more disabilities than others. Rather, we believe that institutional and personal biases and beliefs combine with political pressures to produce a pattern of minority overrepresentation" (p. 100).

Macedo and Marti (2010) also note the impact of bias in special education placement, suggesting that when minority students are over-identified for special education, the group becomes excluded from the "equal education"

(p. 55) offered to the general education students. This exclusion, in turn, affects their prospects for an equal opportunity in society.

Harry and Klingner (2014) comment on the connection between race and the construction of special education: "It should not be surprising that race had become intertwined with the construction of special education, since race has been an essential ingredient in the construction of all aspects of American life" (p. 11).

The unnecessary labeling of children, which assigns them to a socially constructed category within public education, has the effect of blaming students for their educational struggles, expecting less of these students, decreasing their confidence in themselves as learners, and perpetuating a system that promotes inequality within public education, denying many students the right to a quality education.

Shaywitz (2003), along with Morgan et al. (2015), notes that an underdiagnosis of dyslexia in schools denies some students services they need. By contrast, Harry and Klingner (2014) suggest that an overdiagnosis of minority students as having special needs relegates these students to placement in special education, where they are likely to receive lower-quality instruction and lower expectations (Gold & Richards, 2012; Salend, 2016).

Both over- and underdiagnosis are problematic, suggesting a broken system that may do more harm than good for the students who are dependent on this system for services they need. Many students are being left behind not because of their own deficits but because they are victims of a social construct that limits their education.

SOCIAL CONSTRUCTION OF DYSLEXIA AND EQUALITY OF TREATMENT

Historical confusion about the definition and diagnosis of dyslexia illustrates the disparities that result when some children receive educational services while others with similar learning issues remain untreated because of limitations in the way "special education" is provided. The social construction of a disability such as dyslexia may unintentionally promote discrimination and inequity in our education system despite good intentions and efforts to promote equality.

Dyslexia is the most common special education diagnosis within the category of learning disabilities, with 80 percent of learning disabilities reflecting reading struggles (Fletcher et al., 2007; Lapkin, 2014; Shaywitz, 2003). Although reading struggles have been documented as far back as the seventeenth century, diagnosis and treatment remain problematic today (Pullen, 2016; Shaywitz, 2003).

The history of dyslexia provides evidence that this is not a new condition. Successful instructional strategies for teaching reading to the child with dyslexia are well researched but underutilized. Although the definition of dyslexia has evolved, the diagnosis remains elusive for many children, despite scientific advances that allow for clear diagnosis and the availability of instructional strategies that can help these students break the reading code. Furthermore, inequities exist within the population that receives educational services for dyslexia and in the environment and the kinds of services that students receive.

History of Dyslexia

Difficulty with reading is not a new phenomenon; it was documented as early as the 1600s (Shaywitz, 2003). The early cases involved adults who suffered neurological damage from strokes and, as a result, lost the ability to read. In 1877, Adolf Kussmaul, a German neurologist, coined the term *Wortblindheit* ("word blindness") to describe a difficulty with reading (Wolf, 2007). At that time, people with reading difficulties were often referred to ophthalmologists for treatment. Kussmaul also noted that word blindness was not correlated with intelligence but, rather, related specifically to difficulty in recognizing and reading words (Shaywitz, 2003; Pullen, 2016; Wolf, 2007)

In 1891, Joseph Jules Dejerine, a French neurologist, noted that a specific area of the brain, the left posterior region, was critical for reading (Lyon, Sally, & Bennett, 2003). This laid the groundwork for future studies and for a growing understanding of dyslexia as neurobiological in origin. In 1895, the Scottish physician James Hinshelwood noted that word blindness was unrelated either to sight or to cognitive abilities. As he observed many patients who excelled academically but struggled with reading, he came to understand that "congenital word blindness," as he called it, was a specific problem in learning to read that was unrelated to other cognitive functions (Pullen, 2016; Shaywitz, 2003, p. 16).

In this view, a child who is considered cognitively slow in all areas would not be diagnosed with congenital word blindness. Hinshelwood also emphasized the importance of early detection to help children to read, noting that children were often blamed for being lazy when in fact the problem was congenital word blindness (Pullen, 2016; Shaywitz, 2003).

In 1887, the German ophthalmologist Rudolf Berlin coined the term *dyslexia* to "refer to what he perceives as a special form of word blindness found in adults who lose the ability to read secondary to a specific brain lesion" (Shaywitz, 2003, p. 15). For a complete lesion, leading to a total inability to read, Berlin used the term *alexia,* whereas *dyslexia,* the term he used to describe a partial lesion, refers to "great difficulty interpreting written or printed symbols" (p. 15).

The idea that reading difficulty is correlated with the understanding of sounds as they related to symbols dates back to Lucy Fildes, a reading researcher. In 1921, Fildes attributed reading struggles to "problems in the auditory system" (Wolf, 2007, p. 173). As Wolf describes Fildes's discovery in relation to our current understanding of dyslexia, "Children with problems in reading were not able to form auditory images (these are similar to our notion of phoneme representations) of sounds represented by letters" (p. 173).

In 1944, Paul Schilder, a neurologist and psychiatrist, discovered that struggling readers could not relate letters to sounds nor could they "differentiate a spoken word into its sound" (Wolf, 2007, p. 173). This early work set the stage for the current understanding of reading struggles as the "inability to process phonemes within words" (p. 173).

More recently, the use of functional magnetic resonance imaging (fMRI) has allowed researchers to map brain activity, revealing differences in brain activation between children with and without dyslexia (Gabrieli, 2009; Pullen, 2016; Wolf, 2007). Using fMRI, scientists can watch the neural systems at work as a child translates letters into sounds while reading. Through observations of readers with and without dyslexia, scientists have discovered that "[t]he core problem in dyslexia is phonologic: turning print into sound" (Shaywitz, 2003, p. 87).

With this new information, Shaywitz notes, researchers developed treatment for children with dyslexia that would give these children the potential to "reach adulthood feeling confident and able to achieve their potential" (p. 89). But although new research findings have made it easier to diagnose dyslexia, its cause remains a mystery (Hoeft et al., 2006; Moats & Dakin, 2016).

Inequities in the diagnosis and treatment of dyslexia have been observed since the early years of diagnosis. For example, Edward Nettleship, an early-twentieth-century ophthalmologist, noted that word blindness was more easily identified in children of "well-educated" parents (Shaywitz, 2003, p. 23). Observing these inequities, Nettleship advocated for equal treatment for all children.

This history reveals some long-held understandings of dyslexia that foreshadow many of the challenges that remain today. Children with reading difficulties are still identified as "lazy," diagnosis continues to be problematic, treatment continues to be delayed, and inequities in treatment persist (Shaywitz, 2003).

Definition and Diagnosis

As described earlier, the German ophthalmologist Rudolf Berlin was the first to use the word *dyslexia*—a combination of *dys* ("abnormal") and *lexia* ("words" or "language") (Pullen, 2016, p. 26). Dyslexia results from a disruption in the neural circuits in the brain that are used for coding language, affecting a person's ability to read, spell, retrieve words, articulate words, and remember facts (Pullen, 2016; Shaywitz, 2003). Although other terms, such as *reading disability* and *learning disability,* are often used to describe this struggle to learn to read, Wolf (2007) prefers the term *dyslexia* because of its historical roots, while also noting that how we label the problem is less important than gaining an understanding of how to diagnose and treat it.

Shaywitz (2003) distinguishes between *developmental dyslexia* and *language-learning disability.* Both disorders originate at birth, but "in developmental dyslexia the phonologic weakness is primary, other components of the language system are intact" (p. 140) and intelligence is not affected. In language-learning disability, by contrast, "the primary deficit involves all aspects of language, including both the sounds and the meanings of words" (p. 140), and verbal intelligence may also be affected. In this book, the term *dyslexia* is used to refer to developmental dyslexia.

Dyslexia, as defined here, represents a problem with reading that has nothing to do with intelligence. It is a "weakness within the language system, specifically at the level of the phonological module" (Shaywitz, 2003, p. 41). English words are made up of forty-five phonemes in different combinations. The brain needs to break words into phonemes before they can be processed by the language system. A reader must convert letters into sounds and understand the smaller sounds of phonemes.

To become a reader, a child must develop phonemic awareness. Children with dyslexia, however, have difficulty understanding phonemes. They do not understand the "internal sound structure of words" (Shaywitz, 2003, p. 44). A deficit in phonological process interferes with the ability to decode, which prevents word identification.

Reading difficulties such as dyslexia are not uncommon. Currently, learning disabilities account for 50 percent of all students identified in special education, and 85 percent of those identified with a learning disability are diagnosed with dyslexia (Pullen, 2016).

According to Frankel (2009), dyslexia affects one in ten children in Britain, where it is the most common reading disability. Shaywitz (2003) notes that dyslexia is a worldwide condition, with reports of word blindness in the early twentieth century in Great Britain, Holland, Germany, France, various South American countries, and the United States. Dyslexia "knows no boundaries, neither geographic nor ethnic nor intellectual" (p. 31). Shaywitz also emphasizes that dyslexia is found all over the world, regardless of the alphabet that is used.

These statistics may not be surprising when one understands that reading, unlike vision and speech, is a cultural invention developed relatively recently in evolutionary history. Vision and speech are genetically programmed and therefore are passed on from one generation to the next, so that it is natural to learn to speak and to see (Wolf, 2007). But, Wolf notes, "We were never born to read" (p. 3).

There are no genes specific to reading. Like other cultural inventions, it has to be learned by each new brain. Every time the brain learns a new skill, the neurons in the brain make new connections, which change the brain. For example, learning Chinese creates different neuron pathways than learning English does. No neural pathways exist for reading at birth. Rather, we are able to learn to read because our brain can create new neural pathways within its existing structure (Wolf, 2007).

Shaywitz (2003) notes that new research divides groups of poor readers into two distinct categories based on information from fMRI. One group includes the "classic" dyslexic, who is "born with a glitch in his posterior reading systems. This group has higher verbal abilities and is able to compensate somewhat—improving in accuracy but remaining slow readers" (p. 85).

The second group develop into poor readers as a result of a disadvantaged reading environment, either at home or because of poor instruction in school. "In this group," according to Shaywitz, "the wiring for the posterior reading system may have been laid down early on but never activated appropriately; the system is there, but it is not functioning properly" (p. 85). This group, like the first group, will remain slow readers, but they will also struggle with accuracy.

The current widely accepted definition of dyslexia evolved from previous definitions and was adopted by the board of directors of the International Dyslexia Association (IDA) and by the National Institute of Child Health and Human Development in 2002. Many state laws have also adopted this definition (International Dyslexia Association, 2016):

> Dyslexia is a specific learning disability that is neurobiological in origin. It is characterized by difficulties with accurate and/or fluent word recognition and by poor spelling and decoding abilities. These difficulties typically result from a deficit in the phonological component of language that is often unexpected in relation to other cognitive abilities and the provision of effective classroom instruction. Secondary consequences may include problems in reading comprehension and reduced reading experience that can impede growth of vocabulary and background knowledge. (Lyon et al., 2003, p. 2)

This definition is significantly different from previous definitions, and some aspects of it remain controversial. It labels dyslexia as a specific learning disability, thereby creating a distinct category for this type of reading struggle. And in describing dyslexia as having a neurobiological origin, this definition acknowledges the findings of fMRI research, which has identified the neural pathways that differentiate people with dyslexia from those without the disability (Lyon et al., 2003).

One of the most significant changes in the current definition is that it attempts to address the controversy about the use of IQ discrepancy testing as an indicator of learning disability. The idea of "unexpected" academic difficulties suggests a need to measure "unexpected." Historically, comparing IQ scores to other academic achievement tests, commonly referred to as *discrepancy testing,* satisfied this measurement, which assumed that an average person's IQ and reading achievement could be correlated (Shaywitz, 2003).

Today, based on the 2004 IDEA, this IQ discrepancy is no longer required for identification of dyslexia (Wright & Wright, 2015). Instead, schools are encouraged to use Response to Intervention (RTI), an approach based on universal screening of children in the general education classroom. The IQ discrepancy model has been criticized for cultural bias in testing as well as for the requirement that students demonstrate failure in order to get an evaluation—a requirement that had the effect of delaying a diagnosis (Pullen, 2016).

According to both Shaywitz (2003) and Wolf (2007), a clear definition of dyslexia, along with scientific advances that use technology to identify the brain characteristics associated with dyslexia, should facilitate diagnosis, removing much of the doubt about which students should receive services for dyslexia. For many students, however, diagnosis and treatment remain problematic.

Inequity in Diagnosis and Treatment

As with Nettleship's observations in the early 1900s, Shaywitz (2003) and Morgan et al. (2015) contend that today, children from poor families are more often overlooked and not treated for reading difficulties compared to children of wealthier parents. Shaywitz identifies problems with treating students with dyslexia relating to late diagnosis, no diagnosis, and poor quality of services.

Early diagnosis of dyslexia aids in remediation. Yet even with the use of RTI, many students are still not diagnosed early. Although the discrepancy model is criticized for waiting for students to fail, RTI has been questioned for keeping students between Tier 1 (high-quality classroom instruction, screening, and group interventions) and Tier 2 (targeted interventions), which could lead to a delay in diagnosis (Pullen, 2016). Awareness of the value of early diagnosis and treatment is not new, as Hinshelwood noted this in the early 1900s.

The earlier the diagnosis, the easier dyslexia is to remediate, for a variety of reasons. First, the brain is better able to reroute neural circuits when remediation begins earlier. Second, younger children have less to catch up on as their peers continue to move ahead. Third, younger children are less likely to feel defeated or to have developed the deflated sense of self-worth that arises from years of failure and struggles to read (Shaywitz, 2003).

Shaywitz (2003) notes that often children who do not qualify for a diagnosis of dyslexia in schools would still benefit from help in reading. Because these students do not meet the criteria, however, they are left to struggle on their own. This means that the focus on clearly identifying dyslexia can actually limit the learning opportunities available to other struggling readers.

Shaywitz (2003) also found that when students are offered services to remediate dyslexia, the services were often inadequate. As Shaywitz explains, "Children received help for very limited periods of time, often from well-meaning but untrained teachers and with methods that did not reflect state-of-the-art, evidence-based instructional strategies" (p. 35).

Wolf (2007) and Shaywitz (2003) express their frustration with the lack of early diagnosis and treatment for all children with dyslexia, given current knowledge of both diagnosis and treatment. Shaywitz writes, "The greatest stumbling block preventing a dyslexic child from realizing his potential and following his dreams is the widespread ignorance about the true nature of dyslexia" (p. 89).

The social construction of special education is an example of the ways in which the biases of the larger culture may constrain and limit student learning. Special education, designed to help struggling learners, may instead be the cause of student failure as a result of under- or overdiagnosis, the use of detrimental labels, or the influences of racism, classism, and sexism on the services students receive.

Special education is based on a deficit model, providing students with an education that may be "special" but is often not helpful and sometimes even harmful (Gold & Richards, 2012; Harry & Klingner, 2014). This deficit model assumes that for children to receive services they may need in order to learn, they must first be given a label that identifies the problem as existing within the child (Crawford & Bartolome, 2010). This model of blaming the child is not only archaic but also ineffective in promoting student learning. All children can be provided with an appropriate education without having to submit to labeling and testing to prove that a special need exists.

This book examines ways in which students who were blamed, unmotivated, and academically unsuccessful in one educational setting had their educational lives altered when they entered a school that no longer blamed them for their disability but, instead, found ways to teach to them so they could find success. It is this environment to which all students should have access.

Chapter Three

The Serendipitous Pathway

Seeing their child continue to struggle with reading, with little progress, motivated all of the parents in this book to take the role of educational advocates. The paths they followed had many commonalities: They relied on their own parental instinct to guide their choices, often ignoring the "expert" advice from members of the school system. They learned how to "read" their child's behavior as an emotional clue to the child's learning frustrations. They found a person with expertise in special education who introduced them to the Kelsey school. They educated themselves in special education law and the diagnosis of dyslexia. Finally, they acknowledged their own loss of trust in the public school system, creating the final push for them to exit the public schools.

PARENTAL INSTINCT

Parental instinct set in motion the push for advocacy. Many parents knew what "normal" learning or "delayed" learning might look like based on parenting an older child. These parents held on to their belief in their child's ability to learn and achieve, despite test scores and testimony from local school officials that the misguided parent simply was not willing to accept the child's academic limitations. Finally, the parents learned how to "read" and interpret the behavioral and emotional changes in their children that signaled a climax of frustration in their schooling.

Knowledge from Parenting Older Children

For some parents, the knowledge they had gained from raising older children provided them with benchmarks to use in understanding the younger child's learning difficulties. The families of Raya, Beth, Polly, and Tim included older siblings who, for their parents, helped to define the parameters of "normal" and "abnormal." This gave the parents a clue that the younger child might have learning issues.

Raya's mother, Mel, explained:

> We definitely had a hard time remembering letters, learning letters, writing letters; that was a big job in kindergarten. The repetition of all that, you know, we'd show it once and then she would get it, and then she would see it two seconds later and there was no recognition that she had ever seen it. . . . And having an older daughter, I kind of was like—my older daughter couldn't have been *that* spectacular, but this is where we are. So that's kind of when I started clueing into it.

Comparing the capability of her older daughter to Raya's, Mel began to suspect that learning issues were the cause of Raya's delay.

Beth had older grown siblings. Her mother, Mary, recognized issues in Beth's learning to read but felt that school personnel viewed Beth as an uneducable child. They said that Beth tested at a low-average IQ and that Mary expected too much of her daughter. Mary, however, remained confident in Beth's ability. Mary explained that her confidence came from her personal experience in raising two older children: "I knew what to expect with development, you know? I was fairly confident in my abilities as a parent, 'cause I'd already had two children through adulthood. If you make it through the teenage years, you can make it through anything! So, you know, I was confident."

For two of the parents, having an older child with learning issues immediately put them on guard for the younger child. Polly's mother, Leslie, explained, "I saw that the older brother had had some difficulties in school, and I just wanted her to have the advantage of another year of kindergarten. So I . . . requested that and, with a bit of hesitation, was granted that." Leslie continued close monitoring of her child and by first grade, when she was still not reading, asked the school for an evaluation, which later placed Polly on an individual education plan (IEP).

Professionals in the local school system viewed Raya and Beth as functioning well below average, suggesting that their cognitive faculties would hinder their performance. Their parents countered this notion, as each viewed their child as capable of learning beyond the school professionals' expectations. In Polly's case, the school professionals viewed her as progressing normally, but her mother independently identified potential learning issues and advocated for both retention and testing. In all three cases, the parent countered the school system professionals and pushed for what the parent saw as the best avenue for the child's education.

Tim, the youngest of three children, all of whom have dyslexia, benefited from his mother's knowledge of the academic struggles of her older children. Tim, who was eight and a half years younger than his oldest brother, Robert, entered kindergarten just as Robert's disabilities were becoming evident in high school. Tim's mother, Debbie, explained that she initiated early intervention for her middle child, Cally, and for Tim at an earlier age than she had for Robert. Debbie noted,

> They all had early [intervention]. Robert, we didn't start until four years old; Cally, we started at three; Tim, we started at eighteen months. . . . [B]y the third kid, you're like, oh, wait a minute: [the] antenna goes up and you're like, "No." And you find out how many professionals with degrees don't have a clue, because my kids have no behavior problems. . . . They're the kinds that slip through the cracks, because . . . they're going to sit there and suffer and not interfere with anybody.

Aware that her oldest son had graduated from high school with a sixth-grade reading level, Debbie knew her children needed a different kind of education. She presented this knowledge to the younger children's teachers: "I made a big mistake with my older one; this is not going to happen to Cally and Tim. You're going to have to teach them differently." Debbie kept a watchful eye on her two younger children and demanded more from the teachers. She followed her instincts because she knew what her children needed.

Polly, Tim, Raya, and Beth benefited directly from knowledge that their parents had gained through raising older children. These parents built on their core instincts that their children could learn, based on the parents' intimate and consistent knowledge of their child and how he or she behaved in many different situations.

Insight into Intellectual Ability

Nancy's mother, Libby, described simply knowing her daughter's capabilities. She just knew that her daughter could learn:

> When you talk to her, she's very intelligent when talking to you, so you know that she can learn. . . . It wasn't like keeping her back was going to help her. Because she had a disability; I knew she had a disability. You just knew it. And I said keeping her back isn't going to help her. . . . She doesn't get it now and she hasn't been getting it so . . . she has to be learning differently.

Like Libby, Mary felt confident that her younger child, Beth, was capable of learning more than the teachers in the local school system suggested. Mary gained additional confidence from her knowledge of Beth:

They . . . tested her [and] said she had a . . . low-average IQ, but there's a lot of scatter. So . . . but still, she was low-average IQ, so I . . . was expecting too much. I said, there's nothing low-average about this child: I live with this child every day. I'm not delusional; she's an intelligent child. Anyone who asks 400 questions a day to the point where you want to jump out the window . . . about, "Explain this to me, explain that to me," is an intelligent child.

Despite the messages she received, Mary remained convinced that she knew her child best:

[T]hey try to make you think that . . . [your child is] not capable, and you have to trust your own instincts. . . . Every mother knows what their child is capable of . . . and it's not delusional. Every mother knows. 'Cause . . . you're with your child every day; any pediatrician worth their salt will say to you, "If I want to know, I'll ask the mother, 'cause the mother knows."

Evelyn, Mike's mother, also trusted her parental knowledge of her son's cognitive ability, based on his ability to learn chess and build complex structures:

The fact that he could play chess, he could build *amazing* structures, he could . . . go and buy a Lego that was three or four years above his . . . chronological age, and he would sit there with those instructions, and yes, he would get frustrated; sometimes he'd throw them in a heap, but he would go back to that, and he would get that thing made. He would make it. I knew because he could persevere. . . . And he could look at . . . picture cues, he could put stuff together. You know, as a mother, I didn't give up hope.

Raya's parents both rejected information from school officials and chose, instead, to believe in their daughter's ability to learn. Raya's mother, Mel, explained that in one of her meetings with school district professionals, they informed her that she and her husband held unrealistically high expectations for their daughter. Raya's test scores came back low, and Mel found it difficult to attend the IEP meetings and hear consistent reports of low scores. Yet despite the disappointing test scores and the opinions of school officials, Raya's parents refused to accept a dismal outlook for their child. Mel explained:

It was frustrating as a parent to go through [the meetings] because their test results would come back and they would say, "Well, you know, she's in the fifteenth percentile for *this*. . . ." And my husband, in particular . . . said, . . . "Would . . . you be happy with these percentiles if this was your child?" He's like, "This is a comparison of kids that basically have no schooling or no support, and . . . you know . . . the family life can be tragic, and . . . here we are fully supporting her, and you're saying that this is OK that she's in the fourteenth percentile." And they basically looked at my husband and said, "Well,

you're looking for a Mercedes, Mr. Darby, and we're offering you a Chevy."
And he said, "Damn right, I want a Mercedes, and we will be leaving."

This "Mercedes/Chevy" meeting became a turning point for Raya's parents. Mel reported that after this meeting, she and her husband knew they would enroll Raya in another school. With their newfound confidence, Raya's parents were able to ignore school officials' claims that their daughter was doing the best she could.

As another example, Frank's mother, Ella, knew from an early age that Frank had dyslexia. She was confident of this despite the comments from school officials that he had attention-deficit disorder (ADD). Ella firmly believed that the school had misdiagnosed him, and she refused to resort to medicating him for a diagnosis even his doctor had not identified. Ella knew how important it was for Frank to learn to read, and she maintained her high expectations:

> We started kindergarten and I kept asking the teacher faithfully, . . . "Is he delayed? I see other kids doing better than him." "No, he'll catch on, he'll catch on." Well, he'd never catch on, so we tutored all summer long after kindergarten. We started first grade, same thing. "No, he'll catch on." So every year was, "He'll catch on, he'll catch on." . . . They didn't want to admit that he had dyslexia. They kept saying it was ADD. . . . So I brought him to the doctor; he's like, "No, he doesn't have ADD." He goes, "He probably has . . . a learning disability."

Ella explained her frustration that school personnel continued to encourage her to put Frank on medication for ADD. She noted that she often broke into tears:

> They would say to me, "Why are you crying?" I'm like, "This is my son; it's his future. If he can't read, he *has* no future." So I was really pushing. And I was always there and, of course, they would roll their eyes, like, "Here she comes again!" But he's my son, and I'll do whatever I can to help him, so that he's better off in life later on.

In contrast to school professionals who insisted that Frank would eventually learn to read, Ella became frustrated with his lack of progress and transformed herself into an advocate for his education. Throughout his education in public school, Ella continued to raise questions about his progress with school officials. Eventually, she hired an advocate to help get the services she felt he needed.

"Reading" Behavior

The parents in this book learned to interpret their child's behavioral and emotional changes as clues that something was not right in their learning. For example, they observed behavioral changes that emerged around the time when other students were learning to read. Because they understood the reasons behind their child's behavioral changes, these parents were ready to engage in advocacy on behalf of their child.

Mel explained what happened with Raya:

> This is first grade, and [in] the beginning months of first grade . . . she just started getting very emotional. . . . We'd bump into her, she would start crying, it was *not* like her *at all*. . . . [I]t just started escalating from there. I just knew she needed help because she was . . . just becoming sadder. . . . She was sad at school, she didn't like school; she'd come home . . . very grumpy, . . . never wanted to do her homework, doing her homework at night in second grade, . . . just those few pages they get would produce *tears*, and I just was like, "Something is really wrong."

Mel took Raya to a psychologist based on the school's recommendation that psychological problems were preventing her from learning. The psychologist diagnosed Raya with clinical depression. Mel explained that Raya often talked about feeling stupid. As Raya herself put it,

> I remember that I was taken out of my classes . . . every day to do work because they didn't know why I wasn't doing anything right or getting anything done the right way. I'd always be at . . . summer schools and . . . programs, but, like, they didn't know what was wrong. I only had a few friends because a lot of people made fun of me for being, like, dumb.

Mike's challenging behaviors occurred mostly at home. Evelyn, Mike's mother, described her frustration that Mike's behavior was often directed at her, while he showed few behavioral problems at school. Evelyn described Mike's behavior and his anger toward her:

> He was angry. He was . . . pissed off with me, he was pissed off with everybody. But he was really nice to the teacher. He'd come home and I would get a rash. He would just be horrible, horrible! But he'd be nice as pie at school, and the teacher never saw it. Finally one day, I came to pick him up [and] he started . . . he had these panic attacks. You'd drop him off in the playground and there's six hundred kids and he would just start a meltdown. He would just stand there and freeze. The kids would all be lining up, going to the classroom, and he wouldn't move. Or he'd go and hide.

Mike's behavior became extreme. In first grade, he locked himself in the bathroom and refused to come out. Evelyn described removing the bathroom door to get him out. At this point, Evelyn obtained a prescription for anxiety medication for Mike. Yet Mike continued to have meltdowns and became disparaging of himself, especially by fifth grade. Evelyn reported,

> It became a horrendous year, 'cause they were always assigned the homework on Mondays, so he would come home on Mondays and you could guarantee on Mondays, he would have a massive meltdown. . . . Crying, banging his head on the table, puking. "I hate school, I hate myself! I'm dumb! I'm stupid!" All these disparaging things he would say.

Mike recalls how he felt:

> I was just very depressed. I remember, almost every single day I went crying to my room. I was really depressed. I hated my life, I've said that out loud. On top of my schoolwork, I just said, "I'm an imbecile." I wrote all this bad stuff about me.

Evette, like Raya and Mike, had been referred for counseling for depression during her public school years. Evette's mother, Barbara, reported that the school professionals encouraged her to get counseling for Evette because she was "depressed, anxious, irritable—all signs that they thought she was a child at risk at that point."

Evette had been in a self-contained classroom from second grade through fourth grade. When she reached fifth grade, Barbara thought that mainstreaming might be better for Evette. But the fifth-grade mainstream placement brought its own set of problems. Trying to keep up with the work proved impossible. According to Barbara, Evette became more and more despondent. Evette went to great measures to avoid going to school including feigning sickness, ripping up homework, and screaming.

Evette expressed her feelings about going to school. "No! No! No! Please don't make me go! 'Cause it's like torture to go." Barbara described her fears about leaving Evette in public school for the next year:

> I didn't want her going through sixth grade at the middle school, because my fear was that I would lose my child. Because she was just getting more and more despondent about going to school, had nothing positive to say about school, was finding everything she could do to avoid doing her homework and everything, staying up late and not wanting to go to sleep, 'cause if there was a test the next day, she wouldn't fall asleep until almost two or three in the morning because she'd just get so hyped that there was a test the next day, and then would have a bad day doing it. There were a couple of times, though, when she was really, really sad. She says, "I don't want to go. I just want to stay home. Keep me home from school, or else I'm gonna hurt myself." She only threatened it once, but it was enough that I really became concerned.

Frank's mother, Ella, did not comment on any behavioral changes at home but noticed that Frank was getting into trouble at school: "He was frustrated, 'cause he was starting to act out. . . . He got in trouble quite a bit in school." Ella connected Frank's frustration in schoolwork to his "acting-out" behavior in school and knew she needed to find an alternative.

James's parents' concern centered on his increased anxiety about participating in any school activities that might take away from his academics. James refused to participate in special school programming because he feared he would fall behind in his work:

> He refused to take music lessons, because the music lessons were scheduled during school, so he would miss schoolwork. It was just this whole litany of, "I can't do this really fun thing because I'm gonna miss important schoolwork, and then I'm going to have more homework, and then I'm going to be falling behind and then the kids won't like me, and . . ." You know, it's just this whole big mess of "Can't do it," and I was thinking, "OK, when you have a kid who needs that outlet and who's sitting here saying, 'I can't do it,' for all these reasons that really made sense, there's something wrong."

Ardent Advocates

All of these parents maintained confidence in their child and refused to accept school officials' opinions about their child's lack of academic ability or reading progress. Despite dismal test scores, persistent negative messages about their child's abilities and limitations, or assurances that reading skills would develop, each of these parents used knowledge gained from their experiences parenting other children, along with their gut instinct and knowledge of their own child, to keep them on a solid footing as they continued to reject what they were hearing.

What about the outcome for children whose parents may not have the confidence to challenge what they hear from school professionals, or those who may be unaware of the importance of school advocacy? Who advocates for these children, and what happens to their learning?

A public school system should provide access to education for all students, giving every child a chance to succeed, as required by the Every Student Succeeds Act of 2015 (formerly No Child Left Behind). Yet, for these nine students with learning disabilities, acquiring an education that met federal goals and requirements seemed possible only when the child's parents pushed back against professional advice that they believed to be misguided. They found the confidence to do this by following their parental instincts, relying on their personal knowledge of their child, and correctly interpreting their behavior and emotional changes. Based on clues from their child along with their belief in their child's ability, the parents were motivated to become ardent advocates for their child.

EXPERIENCED HELPER

Another commonality among these parents was the involvement of someone who provided information that helped direct them to begin the process that ultimately led them to enroll their child at the Kelsey School. This key person might have been a relative with knowledge of special education, an insider in the school system who had worked at Kelsey, an outside tester, a friend, or a work colleague.

No consistent procedure or process identified these students as dyslexic, nor, once identified, were students consistently directed to a program either within the school system or offered by an outside provider. Rather, this appeared as a more random process resulting from parental advocacy and, often, a serendipitous encounter with a person who might direct the parent to the proper testing, to an advocate, or directly to the Kelsey School.

For example, early in Frank's educational career, Ella learned that her son Frank might have learning issues. When Frank was in preschool, a former Kelsey teacher talked with Ella, "She told me, . . . 'I shouldn't tell you this, but Frank [is] dyslexic.' She goes, 'I know it, I see it.'" Armed with this knowledge, Ella became diligent about getting services for Frank and eventually, on advice from her sister, hired a school advocate when Frank reached second grade.

"Second grade, I got smart, I got an advocate. 'Cause my sister, that's what she ended up doing to get Nolan here [Kelsey]. . . . I didn't think I was getting the services I deserved. And I wanted somebody that knew." With the heads-up from a former Kelsey employee, Ella knew to watch Frank's progress. Based on her sister's experience, she realized that an advocate would be able to help her obtain the needed services.

Eventually, it was the advocate who helped bring about Frank's move to Kelsey: "She said the biggest thing was, we have to prove that they can't educate him. And they're going to try to do everything under their power to keep him here. And we just have to prove that he's not going to advance. So that's basically what we did." With the help of the advocate, Ella was able to demonstrate Frank's lack of progress and to substantiate the need for a different learning environment. Recognizing the important role played by the advocate, Ella now recommends advocates to other parents she knows whose children are struggling:

> Anybody that has learning problems in school, that's the first thing I tell them to go get, is an advocate. 'Cause *I* didn't know. And how *would* I know . . . about any of that stuff? You know, until you experience it, you don't know; and . . . if I can help just one person, . . . and just make their life so much easier . . . my life is a hundred times easier with Frank being here (Kelsey) than Frank being in public school.

Multiple people along Mike's educational journey helped his mother, Evelyn, put the pieces together that culminated in Mike's going to Kelsey. A teacher recognized Mike's challenges and recommended that he get testing outside of the public school system. The teacher suggested outside testing after witnessing Mike behaving inappropriately toward his mother: "'We've got to get him tested . . .' And she said to me, 'You didn't hear it from me, you need to have him tested outside [not within the school system].'"

The testing showed increased levels of anxiety, so Evelyn placed Mike on medication, but his learning issues persisted. Another outside tester eventually diagnosed Mike with dyslexia and recommended the Lindamood Phoneme Sequencing (LiPS) reading program. Instead, the school chose the Wilson Reading System, which Evelyn later discovered was considered less effective than the LiPS program.

To reinforce the Wilson reading program that Mike received at school, Evelyn hired another Wilson tutor when Mike was in fourth grade. This tutor asked whether something else was going on: "She kept saying to me, 'Evelyn, there's a problem. He doesn't get this. I don't know why they move him up. . . . [He] does not have a clue.'" Evelyn shared this with Mike's school reading teacher, who had been praising Mike's progress. But Evelyn persisted, and enrolled Mike in a summer tutoring program.

Talking with another parent outside a tutoring session, Evelyn learned about Joe, a tutor from Kelsey. Although Mike continued in the public school, Evelyn now knew about Kelsey from these sources.

James's parents, Mia and Peter, were also directed to Kelsey by both a school system professional and an outside evaluator, who, in combination, planted the idea of an outside placement. Both Peter and Mia felt that James's evaluation, done by school professionals, lacked sufficient information. A school counselor suggested an outside evaluator and gave them the name of a tester. The private evaluator recommended an out-of-district placement for James. Mia explained their reaction: "We said, 'Absolutely not! We're public school kids. We think that we're gonna be able to make this work.'" Peter added, "We moved to this town just so we could send the kids to this school." Mia explained the tester's reactions:

> So she said, "Well, you might want to find an advocate, just to sort of help you work through the process and understand what your rights are." And so she referred us to an advocate who, again, we were very naïve, and said, you know, "We don't want the team meetings to become confrontational."

Mia and Peter kept James in the public school through his fourth-grade year, trying to find ways to work with the school system and make it successful for their son. Eventually, however, Mia and Peter used an advocate and enrolled James in Kelsey.

For many parents, the process of learning about their child's disability and getting their child to Kelsey centered around knowing about their rights to ask for school testing as well as knowing the differences between school-based testing and private testing outside the school system. The outside evaluator, paid for out-of-pocket by the parents, appeared to start the process by which they came to understand their child's learning issues. Public schools do not traditionally advise parents to make use of private, non-school-based testing.

The parents described in this book learned on their own or from another person that an outside evaluation might offer more assistance in understanding their child's learning issues. Raya's mother, Mel, described the resistance she received from school professionals when the parents inquired about testing. The teacher suggested that Raya was a little delayed but "developmentally on track" and that, given more time, "it would come together." Mel noted, "We bugged them some more, they finally did some testing, but they didn't come up with anything really shocking." After talking with a friend, Mel persisted with outside testing:

> We had her tested outside of school . . . it was like a *complete* red flag; they were like, "She is dyslexic." They didn't even question it. And so we brought that information to the school, [but] they said they thought it was too early to identify her with that type of diagnosis . . . so we just said, "We're out." We just felt like why waste . . . Raya's time at that point?

As a result, Raya entered Kelsey in second grade, the earliest grade possible. For most of these parents, out-of-school testing offered a more comprehensive and unbiased view of their child compared to the school testing.

Evette's mother, Barbara, had a cousin who knew about a testing center out of state. The school psychologist who tested Evette never gave her a diagnosis. Rather, the school psychologist referred to Evette's disability as a "dyslexic-like kind of problem." Evette had qualified for a self-contained classroom, but by the end of third grade she was reading at only a first-grade level. Barbara explained that the testing center had the capability to do a more thorough analysis of Evette's learning issues:

> They go through a complete diagnostic workup, they go through a review, and they do all the different testing, and they even had brain-wave testing and other things that they could be doing, because they were associated with the medical school. I wanted to get away from this school. I wanted to go somewhere that . . . it wasn't being influenced, that their opinion [wouldn't] mean . . . you fit into this mold or something like that. By going out of state like that, I felt that they would give a very true analysis of what was going on with her. And through that, that's when we found out that there was the problem with the auditory processing, about the dyslexia, and they graded it as severe. They said

she was reading at a first-grade level, and that was halfway through fourth grade.

Barbara further explained that although she had known about Evette's reading difficulty since kindergarten, she had trusted the school professionals to find the right solutions for her daughter. However, she came to realize that she had to take the initiative in asking for services from the school system and that she had to find others outside the system who could help direct her. Barbara noted,

> The bottom line has been, until you ask for help, they will not volunteer any additional help until forced to. I have a few friends that are teachers that had told me that they cannot make suggestions that a child needs additional help until the parents ask for it. Even with asking, the parents have to learn on their own or from friends what other options may help. If I did not have these good people [a support group of parents of children with learning disabilities] pushing me to get Evette tested further and make suggestions that she could be doing better with a different learning style, Evette would be struggling in the middle school, a very frustrated, picked-on, and rebellious kid, wanting only to find ways not to do her work and skip school.

Mary went through a long process of trying to understand why her daughter Beth was not learning how to read. This included countering the school professionals who suggested that Beth was incapable of learning. Mary knew the public school teachers were not educating her child, but she did not know where to turn. A coworker helped her find an outside evaluator, who then sent her on to Kelsey:

> I didn't really know what was going on, and I was trying to find out. And it was hard to find out. . . . It took me a long time to figure out that they were more interested in . . . not spending too much money, not spending too much time, than they were in Beth's education. I have two coworkers who had children [at Kelsey]. And I went to them and said, "What is going on? What do I do?" And . . . Deborah [Mary's coworker] said to me. You need to reject this [the IEP], and get an independent evaluation[,] . . . which is what I did.

Mary was shocked by the tester's advice:

> So when I went back, for the post interview, . . . she said: "You need to get her out of the school system *today*. Not tomorrow—today. I'm calling the Kelsey School *today*."
> I go, "Huh?"
> She goes, "If you have to go to a hearing, and you can't afford to pay me, I'll testify for free."
> I'm like, "What?"

She goes, "This is pretty appalling. . . . This borders on child abuse, what the school system has done to this child." And I wasn't prepared for that; I was prepared for her to say, "Oh, she needs this, that, and the other thing."

The tester directed Mary to Kelsey and validated her own perception that her daughter's needs were not being met.

Polly's mother, Lesley, attended Polly's third-grade meeting at the beginning of the year and discovered that Polly was reading two grades below grade level. Lesley knew that Polly struggled with reading, but she had had no idea of the extent of her daughter's difficulties. She went to the school psychologist for advice, and the psychologist, a former Kelsey employee, suggested she enroll her daughter at Kelsey.

Later, Lesley learned that school officials did not approve of her suggestion. Lesley reported how this recommendation happened:

They didn't appreciate her saying that [suggesting a placement at Kelsey]. She was kind of in her private-practice mode of advising people of what they thought was the right thing for their child, not in the "I'll protect the school district" mode. . . . So it wasn't like she could . . . be on . . . *our* side. She couldn't.

For all of these students, a person who provided information, guidance, or a suggestion opened the pathway to Kelsey. Without this direction, which often came about through serendipity, it is unclear what these children's destiny would have been. The question remains: What happens to those children whose parents do not have such experiences?

SELF-EDUCATION

The parents described in this book educated themselves about learning disabilities, special-education law, in-school testing, and the IEP process. One parent learned how to represent her child's case legally. As they sat through IEP meetings and tried to make sense of their child's struggles, parents pursued their own answers. This education took the form of doing online research, reading books, and hiring an advocate who educated them about their rights. These parents wanted answers, and they identified ways of finding them.

Mary explained her process:

I started hitting the computer; I was spending six hours a day reading LD [learning disability] online, Wright's Law; I was going everywhere. I went on Wright's Law, and he says in there, how to read your IEP. And . . . it's a thirty-two-page document, and I went over it page by [page]. . . . He said, "You're going to have to read this, probably four or five times before you get it," right at the top paragraph, but go over it, paragraph by paragraph with your IEP in your hand . . . do it . . . and I did it. It took me a couple of days. He says, "It will show you from IEP to IEP, from evaluation to evaluation, if you have regression, . . . by going through these statistics, the data, the testing[,] . . ." which I did, . . . for most parents, the testing is intimidating. And so, I went through it, I'm like, "Oh, my God! This is *so* awful." I mean, regression in every single area. Every single area.

Once Mary understood the IEP and evaluations, her suspicions became reality. Her daughter was not learning. She found a friend who referred her to an out-of-school evaluator to get more information.

Mel, Raya's mother, became frustrated with the lack of response she received from the professionals in the school system when she asked to have her daughter tested. She talked to a neighbor and then commenced her own search online into special education regulations:

I just was like, this is so weird[;] . . . there's definitely something going on with Raya, but every time we go in they don't want to test her. Then someone who had had a child on an IEP was like, "Mel, they *have* to. . . . It is a *right* of yours." I said, "It is?" I said, "Where did you read *that*?" . . . So then I started going online and I started reading all those rules about laws and I was like, "You're right!" And we *could* have fought for them to pay for the neuropsych, 'cause I think they're required also . . . if we demand *that.*

Evelyn's education about dyslexia happened by chance. While waiting for an older daughter's dismissal from school every day, Evelyn began borrowing books from the parent library. This self-education gave her the information she would need to help diagnose her son:

Over the years, I've borrowed lots of parenting books, and one of them that I borrowed very early, before I even had Mike, was on dyslexia. . . . And . . . I learned about sensory, and I learned about executive functioning, and I'm looking at it like, "Oh, no, no. Can't be." And . . . as more time went on, I . . . revisited these books, and I could see Mike; he didn't fit typically in any pattern, but he definitely [fit] this dyslexic pattern. . . . And I can't even recall what book it was, but it certainly noted that if . . . left-dominancy was . . . apparent before they were a year old, it was very likely that they would be dyslexic. . . . The second year . . . it started to come together, and I kept saying to the teacher, "Do you think he's dyslexic? I think he's dyslexic; do you think he's dyslexic?"

With knowledge gained from her reading, Evelyn questioned the teachers at the school regarding Mike's progress. Evelyn kept a watchful eye throughout Mike's schooling keeping the diagnosis of dyslexia current in her thinking. Evelyn learned that Mike needed the LiPS reading program, but the school offered the Wilson program.

Evelyn explained why she did not insist on the LiPS program: "By this stage, I'm not educated enough to know . . . what's going on, so we are flogging this dead horse, so to speak. Mike now has a tutor two days a week after school." Evelyn subsequently educated herself about different reading programs that appeared to be a better match for Mike, and became increasingly insistent as she gained confidence about what would be the right program for his learning needs.

Debbie educated herself about learning issues as well as the law. She attended seminars on a variety of subjects and, together with a friend, taught herself how to win the legal battle to get her children the out-of-district placement that she felt they needed. Debbie explained that educating herself by attending seminars gave her the knowledge to interpret test scores:

> I'm going, "Oh, gee. There's a twenty-point discrepancy between his perceptional and his verbal comprehension; isn't that significant?" And Cally had a twenty-five-point difference. So I'm like . . . these are things that, when I saw those before, no one explains them to you, and you look at them and you go, "Oh, whatever that means."

In addition to educating herself about her child's disability, Debbie taught herself how to represent her case legally, with the help of online information and advice from a friend: "And she has one year of law school, my friend, and so . . . it's online how to do it, but it's really involved! And you got to do everything exactly how they said, . . . anyway, . . . we won that decision."

Other parents became educated through hiring an advocate who informed them of their rights and how the IEP should be followed. Ella described the value of the advocate, who came to all the IEP meetings: "She was wonderful; she knew that system like . . . the back of her hand. I mean, we would go to meetings, she's like, 'Oh, no, you can't do that.' And they'd look at her. And they knew she was right."

Many of the parents pursued their own education in the terminology, language, and rules of special education. They learned about their rights in the writing of an IEP and under disability law. Debbie was the only parent who also studied legal representation.

These parents took ownership of the responsibility to learn about their child's schooling. They took this education upon themselves in order to discover the root causes of their child's difficulties, to know how to ask the right questions, and to know how to push for services. Evelyn had a note attached to the front of her notebook that contained all of Mike's records. It read, "It's your responsibility to educate our child; it's our responsibility to ensure you do it." Although Evelyn did not remember where this quote had come from, she noted that she lived by it.

The parents felt the need to educate themselves or find an educational advocate to increase their knowledge of their child's disability, the special education system, and their rights. Both Evette and Tim have fathers who have dyslexia, as is true of at least one parent of many children with dyslexia. Dyslexia is a genetic trait and therefore does run in families (Shaywitz, 2003). These parents often continue to struggle with reading as they did in their own childhood.

In this book, it was the nondyslexic parent who pursued education about learning disabilities and special education, and who became the primary educational advocate for their child. The question remains, what about children whose parents are illiterate, have minimal reading skills, do not speak English, cannot afford to hire an advocate, or lack the social and cultural capital needed to advocate for their child? Would their children be at a disadvantage in school compared to other children whose parents have the ability to self-educate?

The concepts of *social capital* and *cultural capital* may play a role in these parents' relative advantage in getting their child to Kelsey. The French sociologist Pierre Bourdieu (1977) defines *cultural capital* as "[i]nstruments for the appropriation of symbolic wealth socially designated as worthy of being sought and possessed" (p. 488). Bourdieu and Wacquant (1992) define *social capital* as "the sum of the resources, actual or virtual, that accrue to an individual or a group by virtue of possessing a durable network of more or less institutionalized relationships of mutual acquaintance and recognition" (p. 119).

In other words, *cultural capital* refers to the parents' match with the dominant culture, which allows them to participate more fully in the school. "Cultural capital includes parents' large vocabulary, sense of entitlement to interact with teachers as equals, time, transportation, and child care arrangements to attend school events during the school day" (Lareau & Horvat, 1999, p. 42). *Social capital* gives parents the confidence to question school authorities and provides social connections that help parents know where to get answers (Harry & Klingner, 2014; Lareau & Horvat, 1999).

Parents who are White and have a middle or upper socioeconomic status have more social capital than Black parents or parents from a lower socioeconomic class in schools (Harry & Klingner, 2014; Lareau & Horvat, 1999). Harry and Klingner (2014) noted that even in schools that had predominantly Black students and Black faculty, Black parents lacked the social capital, such as social connections, and the cultural capital—knowledge of their rights or confidence in their instincts—to advocate effectively for the proper educational environment for their child.

Stanley (2015) concurs, noting that the lack of social capital hindered the ability of African-American mothers from rural areas to advocate for their child as they operated in isolation, not knowing anyone else dealing with similar issues. Stanley also acknowledges the role of cultural capital when parents cannot attend scheduled meetings because of a lack of transportation or because they may work multiple jobs. Finally, Stanley notes that in her research she found that mothers felt discouraged by the ways in which school personnel devalued their knowledge and made negative assumptions about their intellect.

Nord and West (2001) measure social capital in terms of parent educational expectations and shared educational activities. A higher level of parent involvement is correlated with higher levels of social capital. These authors note the direct correlation between parent involvement in school and parents' education level. As the parents' level of education increases, their involvement in school also increases.

Lawrence-Lightfoot (2003) describes the "currency of the classroom" (p. 138), a phrase she takes from a teacher who described the advantage some parents maintain over others in the school system. Lawrence-Lightfoot explains that parents of different racial and socioeconomic backgrounds present differently in school. Privileged parents have high expectations and demand more. They act entitled, aggressive, and determined, and they are strong advocates for their children. Poor parents—"often parents of color or newly arrived immigrants" (p. 109)—do not know how to advocate or to negotiate the school system. They rarely question the teacher, whom they see as the authority.

Shaywitz (2003) comments on the discrepancies in treating students with dyslexia, noting that as early as the turn of the twentieth century, the ophthalmologist Edward Nettleship acknowledged differences in treating and identifying students with dyslexia based on their families' socioeconomic status. Shaywitz explains, "Today, as in Nettleship's time, reading difficulties are often overlooked in children from disadvantaged circumstances. It is not that children from enriched backgrounds are 'over-identified' as reading disabled but, rather, that far too few poor children with the same difficulties are ever noticed, much less treated, for their reading problems" (p. 23).

In a striking example of social and cultural capital, Youn (2015) researched the ways in which social and cultural capital gives students access to the types of educational opportunities that lead to Rhodes Scholarships. Given the effects of social and cultural capital, along with Lawrence-Lightfoot's notion of "currency of the classroom," it appears that certain parents have more opportunity than others to obtain an accessible education for their child.

In this book, of nine White learning-disabled students, families' self-identified socioeconomic status ranged from "working class" and "lower middle class and middle class," to "upper middle class," and "upper class." Most of the families acknowledged their privilege in getting their child to Kelsey.

Five of the parents educated themselves in order to understand how to help their child. This education was one of the factors that helped lead the parent to advocacy, which then opened the way for the child to gain access to an appropriate education. The possession of cultural and social capital may have given these parents the confidence to self-educate and to then use this knowledge to challenge the authority of the school.

LOSS OF TRUST

Many families began their experience in public education with an implicit trust in the system, centered on a belief that teachers would do their best to educate their child and that the child's best interests were at the forefront of their decision making. This degree of trust may vary based on the racial group of the parents. For example, Gasbarra, Johnson and Public (2008) note that Latino parents have an implicit trust of school personnel "to an even greater degree than other parents" (p. 2). Lareau and Horvat (1999) suggest that initially interacting with school with a level of trust is more commonly an experience of White parents than of Black parents.

The authors explain, "Given the historical legacy of racial discrimination, black parents are more likely to begin the process suspicious and critical of the risk of unfair treatment for their children" (p. 42). Howard (2015) concurs, noting a long history of racial discrimination in the public schools.

For the White parents described in this book, a sense of trust appeared to be a given, which broke down over time through a series of interactions and experiences that pushed parents into advocacy. Parents came to realize that school personnel were not going to address their child's needs, either because they held differing views about the child's ability, because they lacked the skills necessary to provide the proper services, or they were worried about keeping their own jobs.

Mary explained her frustrations and her loss of trust:

> My issue was, I didn't really know what was going on, and I was trying to find out. . . . And you couldn't trust them to tell you, 'cause they weren't telling you the truth. . . . But why doesn't everyone in education do what they're supposed to do? . . . When you go into education, isn't it because you want to teach children, you want to help children? I guess that is naïve on my part. That's the thing that bothers me the most, even more than the money, though the money bothers me!

Mary expressed her frustration in a letter to the mayor, who then contacted the special-education director, who convened a meeting. Mary described this meeting:

Not one teacher looked at me the whole meeting; they were all looking at the special ed. director, because they were nervous. [*Whispering:*] "My ass is on the line.". . . they couldn't care less about what Beth's needs were, 'cause they were just wanting to make themselves look good. I was foolish enough to think that in the school system, they want to help your child. And they don't . . . they're just trying to get out of it the easiest way they can. To me that's appalling . . . because I had never felt that way.

Mary's experiences and interactions with school personnel eroded her trust that the professionals were competent and willing to do what was necessary to help Beth learn to read.

Evelyn, Mike's mother, described her gradual loss of trust as she fought for her son's education. In one meeting with the reading specialist from the school system, Evelyn attempted to discuss the coordination between the outside tutor and the reading specialist but found the reading specialist defensive. Evelyn described the meeting:

She wanted total control. [I told her,] "You will never get total control. This is my child, and my child can't read, and it's my job to make sure he learns to read. You can't provide everything he needs here in this school; I need to go outside and make sure he gets everything he needs." So, she didn't like me in that way right from the start because I guess I was . . . This is my kid; my kid's falling apart.

James's parents were committed to public education. Even when the neuropsychologist recommended an out-of-district placement, they remained convinced that the school could help James. At first, on the advice of school personnel, who identified attentional issues as the likely cause of James's reading difficulties, James began medication for ADD. But he continued to struggle with reading, and it became clear that something else was causing James's reading difficulties, and his parents' confidence in school personnel began to erode. They questioned the ability of the school professionals and doubted that the professionals really understood their child. When some school professionals told them that their child lacked intelligence, James's parents, in turn, found themselves questioning the intelligence of the professionals:

The fact that somebody could sit there and say, "He's not smart," and not have anybody else in the room say, "Whoa! Whoa! . . ." You know . . . people don't go from being smart to being dumb. People don't go from having a language disability to having attentional issues [back] to having a language disability. . . . It was so obvious at that point, and we felt stupid; we felt, OK, we've been listening to these clowns for *three years,* and it finally took [someone saying] something totally off the wall like that for us to realize these people did not have a clue.

James's father described how an e-mail exchange with a teacher eroded his trust in that teacher as well:

> We questioned in an e-mail, and she wrote back and listed all her degrees, and her years of experience. And I looked at that and said, "OK, I know in *my* business, when somebody has to resort to what their degrees are, they don't have a clue!"

As James's parents began to question the ability of the school professionals, they also came to realize that programming offered by the school would not accommodate James: "I think in hindsight, we should have been pushing way back on the school for making them responsible for what it was they were providing him, not, you know, 'We're giving him a box; he wants a circle.' 'Well, if he's asking for a circle, he probably needs a circle.' But we didn't . . . we weren't there yet."

James's parents had enrolled their son in public school with confidence that he would get the education he needed. Even when issues started to arise, they maintained their faith in the school personnel until, after repeated meetings, they began to question the abilities of the school personnel and the school programming to provide the services James needed.

Libby, Nancy's mother, described a meeting in which she felt the school personnel were trying to trick her into believing that her daughter was actually doing well:

> I sat at a meeting, and oh, of course, they had *everybody* there: all the teachers, the principal, the guidance counselor, . . . a psychological counselor. . . . And . . . I'm sitting there and I'm like, "Oh, well. This is it; this is the bullying again." And they're telling me how great she is, and . . . what she's doing, and [that] she's progressing, she's really . . . catching on. And then I saw the middle school principal wink down to the special ed. director. It was like, "We've got them in the bag." That was it! I hired a lawyer.

Mel, Raya's mother, explained that they knew enough to question the education her daughter was receiving in the public school system, but she also realized that some parents are more trusting, not knowing that they need to question, and that this can become a problem: "I mean the public school kind of put us forward with outside testing and tutors and then ultimately applying here [Kelsey]. . . . It's just sad, . . . I feel sad for families that just kind of think that they're going to be taken care of under the system."

The parents in this book entered their children in the public school system trusting that teachers would educate their child. Their experiences dealing with school personnel who appeared unprepared to teach their child and seeing their children struggle as learners led them to question this trust and became a catalyst that drove these parents to push for change. In some cases, parents doubted the teachers' skill level; in others, the issue was the programming offered by the school system. Lacking trust, they stepped in as their children's advocates, first pushing for services within the district and then, eventually, advocating for an out-of-district placement.

Meier (2002) describes trust as a cornerstone of education. She believes there are many levels of distrust associated with the public schools, from parents' distrust of teachers to an overall distrust with the school system as a whole. She finds evidence of this distrust in the decisions of outside authorities to mandate standardized testing and to dictate other policies and procedures. Yet all of the parents who appear in this book began with a trusting relationship, which eroded over time as a result of their children's experiences.

Stanley (2015) notes that the Individuals with Disabilities Education Act (IDEA) mandates that parents and school personnel work collaboratively to support children with disabilities. But when parents cannot trust teachers and other school personnel, it is impossible to build such a collaborative relationship, which is key to a child's success in school. Hopson and Lawson (2011) suggest that creating a trusting environment in a school is key to a student's academic performance. Without this trust, parents felt they had no choice but to pursue another placement.

Meier (2002) also discusses another kind of trust that is often denied in school: trust in the idea that humans want to learn. The parents represented here maintained this type of trust in their children; in part, it was this trust in their children's desire to learn that prompted them to reject information from professionals in the school district and then to advocate for their children. However, they witnessed this lack of trust in school personnel, who often viewed their children as lazy and uninterested in learning. Stanley (2015) observes that school personnel often do not trust that African-American mothers care and want to be involved in their child's education.

The trusting relationship, Meier (2002) contends, propels education forward; without trust, education cannot advance to its fullest degree. Meier suggests that this trust must be earned. In the case of the parents in this study, once this trust was broken, the parents took over the educational program for their children—a step that often led to an adversarial relationship with school system personnel.

Public education law gives every child the right to an education. Yet, as the stories of these nine students suggest, this right does not necessarily give children access to the type of education they need for academic success, defined as students' positive feelings about themselves as learners and self-confidence about their ability to learn.

Despite legislation and multiple reform efforts, gaining access to an appropriate education for each of these nine students ultimately relied on the advocacy of their parents. Their stories highlight the arduous, circuitous, and sometimes contentious educational journey each family took before their child finally entered a school that specialized in teaching children with language-based learning disabilities. In the process, these children suffered from anxiety, depression, and diminished self-esteem as they struggled academically to compete with their peers and meet the expectations of their teachers. The story told in this book is not an uncommon one, despite current research that both identifies dyslexia and prescribes specific strategies for teaching children with dyslexia to read (Shaywitz, 2003; Wolf, 2007).

The process by which these children finally gained access to an appropriate education at the Kelsey School appeared serendipitous at times and also relied on parent advocacy that, in turn, often depended on the extent of these parents' cultural and social capital. The parents pursued this goal for their child in the face of numerous barriers, both financial and emotional. Given the paths taken by these nine students, one can only wonder what happens to other students whose families do not have the social and cultural capital to overcome the many barriers that impede access to education for children with learning disabilities—and, in particular, who do not have the good fortune to encounter the types of catalysts that brought these students to an appropriate education.

Is it the parent's responsibility to make sure his or her child is getting an education, or is it the responsibility of the school? If it is up to the parent to ensure that the school does its part—as the note attached to Evelyn's notebook suggested—then the question remains: Do all parents have equal access to the information, privilege, and circumstances that will allow them to be effective advocates?

Chapter Four

Measures of Success

Scores on standardized tests often serve as the accepted measure of student success in school. Educational success, to the families in this book, meant more than just test scores. Overwhelmingly, parents and students noted dramatic changes in students' social and emotional health when they attended the Kelsey School. The children developed a strong sense of self-efficacy, learned how to advocate for their own needs, independently completed assigned work, found meaningful friendships, managed their time and mental energy to participate in activities outside of academics, and improved their behavior. These areas of growth coincided with improved reading scores, suggesting an important interconnection between academics and areas of social and emotional growth.

SELF-EFFICACY

Self-efficacy refers to people's confidence in their own abilities. A strong sense of self-efficacy has been tied to higher levels of motivation and academic accomplishments (Bandura, 1997). Consistently, parents observed and students described feeling more confident in their abilities and having more motivation to learn since attending Kelsey.

Frank

Ella, Frank's mother, described Frank as having become a more confident child since attending Kelsey. She noted, "He's got more confidence. He feels good about himself; he's not afraid to pat himself on the back, where before he just felt like he . . . never fit in."

As Ella explained Frank's transformation, she recalled hearing similar stories from other parents near the beginning of Frank's first year:

> I remember the first meeting [at Kelsey]; 'cause there [were] a couple of other parents that, you know, their kids were first year, and we were all like, who took our kid? Who is this person? 'Cause my kid was just like . . . he went from being such a . . . disruptive, angry person to . . . a very happy child. . . . Totally . . . a different child.

Ella related how Frank's self-efficacy seemed to build as his academic ability grew: "He knows that he can write a sentence; he knows he can write a paragraph, where . . . at [his old school] he didn't know where to begin." Further, she explained, he now does his homework on his own: "He knows what to do. . . . All his homework, he does, I don't help him with any of his homework[;] . . . I know that they don't send home any homework that he can't do on his own."

Frank himself noted, "I went to Kelsey and felt like I was learning a lot more. . . . There was a lot more reading, and recitation was all about work, and you could do stuff."

Once Frank found academic success, his belief in his ability to learn increased, as did his motivation to go to school. Frank described his newfound pleasure in learning: "You can learn a lot more. Instead of sitting there, doing nothing, you actually can do something." At his old school, he explained, he had no interest in learning, but at Kelsey, there are "a lot more things to learn about [at Kelsey]."

Frank's science teacher, Fiona, noted his participation in class:

> For the most part, he's been pretty consistent with . . . his effort and his output. There've been [a] few little dips here or there, if something's going on at home that . . . he might not put the top quality into his homework, but he's a great . . . participant. Usually, he's volunteering to read or answer questions, and depending on the topic.

These positive comments stand in sharp contrast to the litany of negative reports from Frank's previous school, where Frank was consistently described as lacking effort and interest in learning.

Evette

Evette's mother, Barbara, and Evette's teachers all noted marked changes in Evette's self-efficacy since attending Kelsey. Barbara described Evette's newfound confidence in her academic ability: "I think that's one of the things that she never felt until she got to Kelsey, that she was truly a smart kid. . . . She knows that she can get it [her work] done. And she's actually being more helpful around the house now, and everything else, because I think she has more confidence in herself."

Barbara noted that Evette's fifth-grade teacher described her as "lazy and doesn't try hard, and easily gives up" but that this has changed since Evette began attending Kelsey: "[T]he child that would easily give up is gone because now there's a child that wants to learn, and that's the huge . . . difference between the public [school] and Kelsey."

Like her mother, Evette herself noticed her increase in confidence, to which she attributed her active participation in Kelsey activities and events: "I would have never done a panel. I would have never [run] for student council. I would have never done a play, would have never become a cheerleader or anything."

Evette explained that before she arrived at Kelsey, her attitude was "I don't care. I don't plan on doing anything. . . . But now, I plan on doing stuff with my life. . . . '[C]ause now . . . everything got so easy and everything got so smooth and . . . better."

Evette's student advisor, Sally McKay, noted that Evette ran for student council, participated in the Kelsey plays, and helped with student council activities. She described Evette as fitting in with Kelsey, in contrast to her experience at her old school: "You know, things at home in Rogersville [Evette's local public school district] were difficult for her; . . . she always felt the odd man out. . . . [S]he really didn't feel that she was making progress, and she feels now that Kelsey is the place for her, and . . . that she can thrive here."

Evette's teacher Fiona commented on the dramatic change she observed in Evette since the beginning of the year:

> She's *very* eager to please, wants to learn, wants to do the right thing. . . . One thing that kind of struck me at the beginning of the year was, . . . if she made a . . . mistake on her homework or classwork, . . . *or* if I was giving a suggestion on an easier way to do it, she'd get a little defensive and . . . almost try to make excuses for *why* it was wrong. . . . I felt like her defenses were really up, and I'm sure it was probably due to past experiences, . . . that's really changed dramatically.

Throughout the year, Fiona observed, Evette became increasingly willing to accept feedback. She described Evette as "soaking up any strategy that she can." As an example of Evette's enthusiasm about new learning strategies, Fiona described the way Evette told a neighbor about solving division problems using the "steel ladder," a method unique to Kelsey.

Fiona also saw evidence of Evette's increased confidence in her enthusiasm about performing for her class and even for the whole school: "She loves to be at the front of the room explaining a problem and showing her skills and stuff like that. . . . I *love* the strength and courage she has for doing the things that she does, 'cause she doesn't always seem the most secure, but she's not afraid to take a risk, like getting up in front of the entire school."

Maggie Wright, Evette's language arts teacher, noted that Evette often wrote about her academic and social struggles in her old school, contrasting that experience with the success she felt at Kelsey. As Maggie described it,

> [s]he had anxiety about *every*thing [at her old school]. And here, she feels successful and she gets yelled at for going *ahead* in math, instead of falling behind, and she feels . . . I mean, she still struggles socially and stuff, like every middle school kid does, but she's . . . like, "Hey, I'm successful! You know, look at all these things I've done: I'm . . . I have stage fright, and I was in a play."

As recounted by multiple teachers as well as by her mother and herself, Evette's feelings about her ability as a learner changed dramatically while she was at Kelsey. This increased sense of self-efficacy appeared to influence her motivation to learn.

James

James's parents reported an increase in James's self-confidence and self-efficacy during his time at Kelsey. With this new confidence, his parents said, they could now imagine him going to college and on to a professional career: "It's almost like there's a different prism through which he sees himself, because so many of the things that are hard for him are still hard; [but] they're not *as* hard, and the failures aren't as great and the gaps aren't as great."

James's mother commented, "He still has those problems [dyslexia], but those problems aren't important any more. They don't *define* him." James's father added, "He's not going to be the world's best reader, but now he knows how smart he is." Both parents noted that James's new level of confidence allowed him to think about getting a summer job without worrying about his capability: "He's going to be fourteen in April, and he wants to get a job over the summer. . . . There's nothing about any of the jobs that [is] worrisome, in terms of what he can and can't do. I think that sort of self-confidence is from being here [Kelsey]."

Mike

Evelyn noticed a dramatic change in Mike's self-efficacy after attending Kelsey: "He *feels* successful. When he sits down and he talks to you, he is confident about the information that he's telling you, 'cause he's learned something."

Evelyn reported that Mike's confidence in his ability grew as he found that he was able to complete homework on his own and no longer had to rely on his mother to get his work done. He felt empowered by his independence. Mike noted that at his old school, lunch was his "favorite subject," but at Kelsey he enjoyed all his academic subjects. He marveled at his ability to do the work on his own: "It's been a compete change to my life. Back at my elementary school—torture—I had to always depend on my mom to help me do my homework. . . . It's complete . . . it's different, it's amazing, it's the best school I've ever been to in my life."

Raya

Mel, Raya's mother, described Raya's increased self-efficacy since attending Kelsey, as reflected in Raya's belief in her own abilities:

> She knows she can. She never thought she could, and I think *that's* what they [Kelsey School] do: "You can." They empower them. And she's like, "Yes, I can. I can." For her to get a hundred on her quiz[,] . . . I mean, she's just like, "Well, I'm just like my brother and sister now. . . . I'm as smart as you."

Mel emphasized Raya's confidence in her abilities as one of the most remarkable aspects of her daughter's experience at Kelsey: "They just really embrace them with such confidence here [at Kelsey], like she'll say: 'Yes, I am dyslexic, but that doesn't mean that I'm not smart and that doesn't mean I can't learn.'"

Raya noted that being able to read gave her an increased sense of her own ability: "In first grade people were reading Harry Potter books because they were so smart and I'd be reading those cardboard ones with three words on each page, and now that I can read *Twilight* [book series] it makes me feel *so* much better about myself. . . . I know things now and I'm not shy like I used to be and so I can say stuff more, like I can share what I'm thinking and I feel really good about myself."

The students described in this book, as well as their parents and teachers, experienced marked changes in their attitudes and thoughts about their academic ability. These students no longer viewed themselves as incompetent learners. They found success at Kelsey in their ability to do homework and understand the material. They came to realize that having dyslexia did not correlate with an inability to perform academically. Their newfound confidence increased their motivation and interest in learning.

SELF-ADVOCACY

Parents, students, and teachers all observed an increase in students' ability to self-advocate since attending Kelsey. These students learned to ask questions and to express their learning needs as determined by their disabilities. Paul Stanford, Kelsey's public school liaison, noted that for students who attend Kelsey, in addition to gains in academic skills, self-esteem and confidence also "shoot up." He described the development of self-advocacy as a major part of the Kelsey program.

Parents consistently commented on a marked shift in their child's ability to self-advocate since attending Kelsey. They described changes in class participation, particularly the child's willingness to ask and answer questions. Parents also noted an increased sense of security and comfort in the classroom. For example, Mel noted that Raya, who had always avoided asking for help, now has the confidence to speak up when she has a question. Mel explained:

> She is not afraid to ask, and I think she was always afraid to ask questions, like, "I can't read this, can you read this word to me?" or "I don't understand this," because in her eyes that was admitting that she was stupid or she didn't understand it, where now she's so confident, she'll be like, "Well, Mom, can you read this word?"

Students exercised self-advocacy in the way they described their learning needs. For example, Evelyn observed that Mike now understands his own need to focus more and pay attention in class. Evelyn attributes this understanding to the "environment" at Kelsey, which has encouraged him to develop his self-advocacy skills.

As students advance in school, they must increasingly rely on themselves to make sure their educational needs are met. Dyslexia does not go away or get cured. Rather, students must learn how to address their learning needs through self-advocacy. In her research, Olson (2009) interviewed a college graduate with dyslexia who attributed his academic success to his ability to understand his own learning needs and then advocate for accommodations.

ACADEMIC INDEPENDENCE AND IMPROVED ABILITIES

For many students, teachers, and parents, the child's improved reading level and writing skills became the obvious marker of success at Kelsey. In addition, parents noted their child's newly acquired independence in doing their own work as an additional measure of success.

For example, Anna Brush, Raya's teacher, spoke about Raya's improved reading while at Kelsey: "Her reading has made gigantic gains. I mean, last year she was reading at probably . . . a mid-second-grade level for fluency, and this year, she's . . . just about the sixth grade, and she's in the sixth grade . . . she's really closed the gap." Anna also observed an increase in Raya's academic risk taking compared to the previous year, when Raya often cried when the teacher introduced new work.

Patty Ryer, Frank's recitation teacher, noted that Frank began Kelsey as a sixth grader, at a "high-second-grade to low-third-grade reading level." In two years, she observed, he had advanced to a fifth-grade reading level. Frank's student advisor, Erin Stout, reported that Frank had improved in writing as well. She noted that in a small, structured writing class (four students), Frank's writing mechanics had improved, as had his attitude about schoolwork. For Frank, this represented success, given his apathetic attitude toward learning at his old school.

Lesley, Polly's mother, described proudly how she had made the transition from buying books for Polly to borrowing library books, because Polly was now going through books at such a rapid pace. She noted that Polly's reading has advanced "in leaps and bounds," both in silent reading and in reading comprehension.

James observed his own change as a learner. He described his increased interest in writing, which he had previously "hated," and his willingness to read in school. When he wrote a story for homework, he said proudly, "I have the greatest story in the world for this! I came in with three and a half pages; everyone else has one and a half." James added that while he might still prefer to get a book on tape ("I'll be lazy like that"), he no longer tries to avoid reading with teachers: "It's like, 'OK, reading homework, OK, I'll read it.'"

James sees a change in himself, and his student advisor Kelly concurs. She noted that James has "really taken off in terms of applying the strategies that he's learned." James's parents reflected that because he has learned to read, James now participates easily in all sorts of daily activities that he previously might have avoided: "He is able to read menus at restaurants and look up [phone] numbers."

Debbie recalled the first indications that her son, Tim, was starting to find success at Kelsey: "I'll never forget the first year we were here, and we were here about six weeks and we were driving back and he read a sign. He would *never* read out loud to us, and he read the sign to us, just because he wanted to show us: 'Look, I'm starting to be able to read.'"

Evette's mother, Barbara, and Evette herself both saw tremendous changes in Evette's reading ability after only a year at Kelsey. Her student advisor and language arts teacher also saw improvements but noted that Evette still had some distance to go in order to read at grade level. Barbara described Evette's reading progress:

I am just amazed how much better she is able to read. Very few hesitations, much clearer with how she pronounces her words. . . . [T]hat's just been huge. This is the chair that we brought down when the Christmas tree was there. She wanted the chair put there so that she could sit and read. . . . I've been a reader all my life; I love to read, and that now she has access to reading, and gets enjoyment from reading, is amazing.

Evette chimed in enthusiastically: "This is my second book this year."

Sally, Evette's student advisor, noted Evette's improvement after just six weeks in the Lindamood Phoneme Sequencing (LiPS) program during the summer: "We tested her . . . before the summer and she was reading at the 1 percent [level]—the equivalent of grade 1.3. By the end of the summer we tested her again and she was [at] 22 percent. So there was improvement, and it was an indicator that the LiPS program was for her." While acknowledging Evette's newfound joy in reading and her progress this year, Sally cautioned that Evette still reads significantly below grade level and has "a lot of catching up to do."

Mike noted his own increased interest in learning since attending Kelsey. He enjoys school now instead of dreading school: "I was not depressed anymore. I'm very excited to learn, which is a surprise . . . 'cause at my old school, . . . I was like, 'Do I have to go?' . . . Even though Kelsey is an extra hour of school[,] . . . the time doesn't really matter here. You always can enjoy yourself on homework, playing chess."

Mary, Beth's mother, described how Beth demonstrated her improved reading at the hearing with her town, as a way of illustrating the dramatic changes that Beth had experienced at Kelsey. Beth had learned to read after only seven months at Kelsey during the academic year plus six weeks in the summer program. This came after six years in the public school system, during which she had not learned to read.

The experience convinced Mary that Kelsey had the program her child needed. As she described it at the hearing: "My child can read now. I don't have to go to a restaurant and read the menu to her. She can read it for herself. If we're going down the street, she points at a street sign, she can read it for herself, she doesn't have to ask me what it says."

Mary added, "Maybe that's not data, but that's tangible things that happen to us every day now that never happened before. I mean, it was like a miracle, her coming to school here. We went from . . . despair to . . . she can read now."

Another measure of success was the children's independence in doing homework. Through years in public school, many of the parents either did the homework for their child or provided many hours of help. At Kelsey, students found success in completing homework on their own, and this experience helped build their self-confidence. Mary, Beth's mother, explained that at Kelsey, they assign homework the students will be able to do.

Mary noted the relief she and other Kelsey parents feel now that their children do homework independently. Describing the new parents' orientation at Kelsey, she noted the anxiety on parents' faces when the headmaster mentioned homework, followed by relief when he said, "We don't want you helping them with their homework, because we don't care what you know. We don't care! You let them do their homework."

Mary added, "It was such a relief to know you're not going to have two hours of crying and fighting and going, . . . 'Yes, you have to do this' . . . . None of that happens anymore."

All of the parents commented that the ability to do their own homework made their children feel better about themselves. Mel noted that Raya had previously felt devastated that her younger brother was able to do her homework while she could not do it on her own. At Kelsey, by contrast, Raya happily completes all of her homework without assistance. Evette's and Tim's mothers both noted that at times their children might ask questions about a word or about spelling, but this is rare. For the most part, they do their homework on their own—a major shift from their previous schooling experience.

Mike reported a major sense of accomplishment at Kelsey now that he could complete his homework without his mother's help: "She [his mother] doesn't even know what's going on, she doesn't know if I have a test anymore, when I do pretty well, I'm like, 'Mom, look at my science test, I got 95,' she's like 'Nice.' . . . And I was very impressed with myself, and I did it all by myself."

Mike and his mother both recalled how many hours Mike's mother had spent working on homework before Mike transferred to Kelsey. They both acknowledged their excitement over Mike's newfound independence. Teacher Maggie Wright observed that all students at Kelsey take pride in their ability to do homework on their own. For most of these students, she noted, this is a new phenomenon. Once, Maggie made a mistake on a homework assignment and was concerned that parents might contact her, but she soon realized that Kelsey students are so proud of their independence that they do not involve their parents:

> The kids here are very determined to do their homework with zero help, so the chances that a parent looked at it are pretty slim, because they're very proud of the fact that they can do their homework on their own. And for a lot of these kids, this is the first time they've ever, *ever* experienced that.

Parents, students, and teachers alike noted significant increases in students' reading and writing abilities since attending Kelsey. They also described students' feelings of pride and success in completing homework independently. Increased reading and writing ability and academic independence constitute additional measures of success for Kelsey students.

SOCIAL GROWTH

Both parents and teachers observed social changes in students while attending Kelsey. Teachers observed how students learned necessary social skills, and parents noted an increase in friendships. Students also commented on the ease with which they made friends at Kelsey. Patty Ryer explained how, at Kelsey, James "learned to be a student." Many students new to Kelsey, according to Patty, need to learn how to sit quietly, listen to the teacher, take out their supplies, and stay in their seats. Some also need lessons in social pragmatics, such as using tissues and understanding personal space. Kelsey teachers use reminders and modeling to help students improve in all of these areas.

Mike, Raya, Nancy, Frank, and Evette all reported finding it easier to make friends at Kelsey than at their old school. They suggested that Kelsey students understood them better because they all shared a common learning disability. Raya explained: "People understand what's going on around them and [that] it's different the way our minds work. We attack problems differently." She noted that conversations with students at Kelsey are easier and are less confusing.

Nancy described cliques in her old school that made social interactions stressful. In comparison, "[a]t Kelsey, they don't have cliques and everybody kind of fits in, so . . . it's like a big, big family." Frank observed that he no longer got into fights with other students. Like Raya, he felt that students at Kelsey understood him better.

Evette felt a connection to other students at Kelsey that she had lacked at her old school. Because of the isolation many students felt at their old schools, either because of daily pullout special-education sessions or because they felt stigmatized by having a learning disability, these students and their parents noted the ease with which the children fit in socially at Kelsey. This became another marker of success.

PARTICIPATION IN OUTSIDE ACTIVITIES

For many students in this story, Kelsey offered a safe place to participate in extracurricular activities such as sports and drama. In addition, the more manageable homework load made it easier for students to participate in town sports teams.

James's parents noted how James benefited from the extracurricular programming at Kelsey, where he participated in both drama and cross-country:

> From a social standpoint[,] . . . he can be on a team. He's never going to be the first person to cross the finish line in a cross-country track meet. He knows that, but he also knows that showing up and competing and trying his hardest is going to get rewarded here. He'd get cut in a week, in [public school]. He *knows* that he can learn to read a script here and perform on stage. . . . He wouldn't even make it through . . . a cold read of a script at a high school audition. There's the academic piece where he needs to be here, but even for the extracurricular activities, he couldn't fully participate . . . in *that* part of school life, without the sort of accommodations that they have here. . . . Drama students get help reading and memorizing their lines, and everyone makes the cross-country team.

Evelyn explained how Mike regained a life outside of school after starting at Kelsey. As a family, they now have time to go out to dinner, go bowling, or visit the science museum. He is able to participate in the town soccer program and a Sunday school church group. The reasonable workload at Kelsey allows Mike time to maintain all of these interests outside of Kelsey—something that was not an option for him in the past.

The ability to participate in extracurricular activities provides Kelsey students with an enriching environment. Without the support they receive from Kelsey staff, drama and some sports might prove too difficult for a child with dyslexia. Frank's mother, Ella, recounted how Frank had had difficulty playing football on the town team because he could not understand the plays. At Kelsey, Frank successfully participated in sports. Kelsey provides a safe and forgiving atmosphere where students feel comfortable participating in extracurricular activities.

In addition, because the workload at Kelsey is tailored to the child's ability, Kelsey students have time to participate in activities after school. This participation proved to be another measure of children's success at Kelsey.

IMPROVED BEHAVIOR

A consistent measure of success reported by many parents was an improvement in behavior once their child started at Kelsey. This included changes in moods along with a decrease in depression and anxiety. Raya's mother noted an observable decrease in Raya's moodiness, with less crying and fewer breakdowns. Frank's, Mike's, and Tim's mothers all observed similar changes in their children, noting the absence of the "meltdowns" or "shutdowns" that had occurred regularly when their child attended public school.

Barbara, Evette's mother, noted that Evette now helped out more around the house.

Mike's pediatrician and therapist both noted dramatic changes. Mike's pediatrician wrote, "I think it's clear that now that he's in a better school environment, the depression and anxiety issues will gradually fade in importance. It's possible we may discover the ADD was mostly secondary to the dyslexia as well."

Soon after, Mike's therapist wrote to Mike's pediatrician: "Mike is doing very well. His depression symptoms have resolved and he has not experienced any anxiety in the past few months. As you may know, Mike is attending Kelsey School and doing quite well academically and socially. . . . His sense of humor has blossomed, making him quite fun to spend time with."

Evelyn also noted her joy in discovering Mike's sense of humor: "We never saw that sense of humor before. . . . It . . . would be there occasionally, but . . . it would be more of . . . a dry thing. But he'll say things now, and . . . he knows he's pulling your chain, he knows that he's going to get a crack out of you."

James's parents explained that because school professionals continually suggested that James suffered from attentional issues, he had had a three-month trial of attention-deficit disorder medication. But the change in school had proved to be more beneficial than any medication in addressing James's issues with focus: "Since he's been [at Kelsey], . . . *yes*, there are focusing issues, *yes*, there are attending issues, but they can be managed and he can be redirected."

James's parents also noted that counseling services were no longer needed. They relayed that the counselor reported, "There wasn't anything inherently wrong with him; he really needed help coping with a bad situation." At Kelsey, James was able to function without medication and without counseling.

While acknowledging that James's issues had not vanished, James's parents found that the Kelsey environment had helped transform him into the student he wanted to be:

> James . . . hasn't transformed into a completely different kid; [he] is just more of the person that he always was, because he's able to thrive by being that person here. He was never going to thrive as the person that he is in that other school. . . . In order for him to succeed at a public school, he would have to be on Ritalin, he would have to be the automaton kid, and he wouldn't be James anymore.

Other parents also noted marked changes in their children's behavior after attending Kelsey. "Shutdowns," "meltdowns," and "breakdowns" all declined. Children who had required medication for depression, anxiety, and other conditions in their previous school setting no longer needed to be medicated. This change in behavior constituted another measure of success for Kelsey students and their families.

It is evident that these children found success at Kelsey according to multiple measures. Parents, teachers, and students all noted marked changes in self-efficacy, self-advocacy, academic independence and ability, social interaction, participation in extracurricular activities, and behavior—for example, expressing a desire to go to school. These measures clearly resonated with parents, students, and teachers alike as important markers that indicated that the Kelsey school had altered the course of education for each child in a life-changing way.

Part II

The Kelsey School

A Model That Works

"The effective school must become an educative setting for its teachers if it aspires to become an educational environment for its students." (Shulman, 2004, p. 334)

"I am a severe dyslexic. I cannot write. That really limits you in what you can do. I wish I had a choice. I went to Kelsey high school for two years at the end of high school, but it was to late." (Ryan Colter, Kelsey School janitor, April 2009)

Chapter Five

Dedication to the Mission

Like many schools, Kelsey has a mission statement, which was developed at the school's inception and appears on the Kelsey website and in its literature. The mission describes the school's commitment to help students with language-based learning disabilities (LBLD) become independent and confident learners both academically and socially. The mission also includes the school's pledge to use a high-quality program based in research and training.

Teachers who appear in this book attest that the mission statement truly does reflect the core values expressed by staff members and provide the common vision that unites the teachers in shared goals. This felt connection to the mission enables teachers to work together for a shared purpose. Kelsey's founder, Anthony Black, wrote the original mission statement in the early seventies along with the board. There were minor adjustments to the wording over time, but the meaning has remained unchanged.

Bert Stack, principal, explained how dedication to the mission pulls the community of teachers together to focus on a central goal:

> My own experience with public schools has often been that teachers get isolated; they often refer to their own turf and their own room and their own material and their own curriculum: "It's my stuff." Whereas here, I feel like everybody buys into the place the way you'd buy into your own house or your own . . . neighborhood, . . . so I always feel there's a sense of sharing, a sense of trying to make everybody better. A lot of that, I think, stems from the mission that it's not about the people who work here as much as it's about the mission.

Bert further noted that the focus for the teachers at Kelsey becomes the mission—their shared commitment to remediating students with language-based learning disabilities—rather than "doing your own thing." At Kelsey, he added, "It's a mission-focused environment; if you're not here because you want to remediate language-based learning disabilities, then you shouldn't be here."

Bert identified the mission as his own reason for coming to Kelsey: "I was looking for a Peace Corps–like experience, something with a clear mission that I could buy into and get involved in. And that, combined with the literacy, was what attracted me to the place."

Staff, quoted in this book, corroborate Bert's description of the faculty. For example, Patty Ryer described how working at Kelsey fit with one of her own core values: "I think that everyone has the right to . . . be a literate member of society. Everybody has the right to read and write, and those who have trouble with that will be severely hampered."

Patty further explained her commitment to helping her students:

> I take it on as a personal responsibility that I'm supposed to help them to advance to whatever their goal is for the following year in their IEP. . . . I make it really clear to them that we're *both* responsible for it, so the homework that they do at home and the planning that I do outside of class hopefully comes together and culminates in a really strong lesson.

In Patty's classroom she shows her dedication to the mission through her commitment, patience, and understanding. For example, she often has to repeat directions over and over, without raising her voice or appearing frustrated. But this does not bother her: "I have a lot of patience for things that are out of the student's control." From her observations of James, Patty was aware that others might interpret his learning style as rude or inappropriate since he does not comply the first or even second time.

> Sometimes the visual piece confuses him, so sometimes if we're doing something and I say, "Eyes up here," or, "Eyes on the board," he may look and then glance away, and I'm OK with that, because I do think sometimes the visual input confuses him. . . . He learns through questioning. He loves to find the exceptions to the rule. . . . And if you don't know that that's the way he learns, it comes across as him just being bratty and trying to point out your mistakes.

Patty knows that students with dyslexia may need repeated cuing and more precise directions than other students require. She understands that these students' questions and comments may be misinterpreted, and she accepts responsibility for teaching them how to manage their disability: "Part of my job is to help [them] to figure out when [asking lots of questions is] appropriate to do, and [when it's] not appropriate to do." On multiple levels, it appears that Patty maintains a commitment to and an understanding of this student population and adapts her teaching to help them find success.

Maggie Wright, a first-year teacher, described the importance of present-ing material so her students understand it. She believes it is her responsibil-ity—not the students'—to ensure that they understand her teaching:

> Three kids in my class don't get it, it's for three different reasons, and I have to figure that out, and solve it using as little language as possible, which is like the ultimate puzzle. It's fascinating. They're going to get it or they're not going to get it, but that's based on what I do, 'cause they're doing the best they can, using what they've got to work with.

At times, Maggie explained, she feels like a failure—for example, when the students don't understand even though they are working their hardest:

> There's some days, when it's like, . . . we have done this activity fifty times, and you can't do it. And it's like, "Oh, my God! I feel like such a failure. This kid cannot do this." I mean, we have done it fifty times, every day for fifty days, and there's certain days that they're just not going to be able to do it. And then they come in the next day, and they've got it down! It's like, that fluctuation in processing speed, that fluctuation in word-recall ability is *unbe-lievable* for some of them. Some are very consistent, but I've got one or two that are just like, they have on days and off days, and they're trying equally hard, on both days.

Maggie's commitment to this student population may come from her beliefs in the importance of learning to read:

> And to think about these kids: How are they going to take their driver's license test if they don't get what they need to get here? If I don't take this time . . . and every second is *so* precious, because the older they come in, the harder it is, and if I don't take every single second and make it as efficient as possible and teach them as much as I can, then that driver's license test, signing that cell phone contract, buying their first car[,] . . . they're going to depend on others; they're not going to be able to do it for themselves. And that's just crazy to me. . . . They're going to have to go out on dates and fake it. I mean, they're going to be twenty-two, and they're going to go out to some fancy restaurant and have to order the special every time, because that is orally transmitted. . . . So that's my context within which I am teaching.

Maggie described the new appreciation for different learning styles she developed through working at Kelsey. For example, she is no longer critical of people who make spelling errors in e-mails, and she understands the types of questions people ask at the grocery store:

> I used to be frustrated working in a grocery store when people would ask me what we have, when it was all written right in front of them. And now, I am *far* more forgiving of that. If somebody asks me about something, I don't assume that they can read, and I *never* would have felt like that before.

Claire Jenkens, who has taught at Kelsey since the school's earliest days, reveals her match with the mission statement when she recalls her response to an interview question posed to her by Kelsey's founder, Anthony Black. Although this interview took place almost forty years ago, Claire still remembers his specific question and her exact response.

Anthony asked, "What is your philosophy about how children should be taught?" Claire responded, "Every child has the right to meet his potential academically, socially, emotionally, and physically." She believes her answer must have satisfied him, because he offered her a position.

Over her four-decade tenure at Kelsey, Claire's commitment to this population has not lessened: "The challenge to see students who struggle with writing has kept me at Kelsey these many years, especially those students who do not feel that they can write anything well or anything at all. Kids like James, for example, who are reluctant to express their ideas and have a lot of difficulty conforming to certain expectations and standards."

Claire described what she enjoys most about teaching at Kelsey:

> It's seeing the kids who have been written off as hopeless, and knowing that they have the ability to do the work, it's just that the approaches that have been used haven't been correct, and that there's an approach here that will work. . . . Some kids start at a very low level, and then, given a year or two, the change is incredible. Seeing this change is a miracle because they've been written off as failures in other educational settings. I love the challenge of seeing kids achieve in this program and be able to move on with their lives and be successful.

Claire's stated commitment to teaching this student population upholds Kelsey's mission to help these students reach their potential. Claire also conducts her own research and presents at many conferences. In this way, she further supports Kelsey's mission of research and outreach, to allow other teachers to learn how to work with this population.

Multiple veteran staff members commented on their fulfillment in seeing students find success at Kelsey. This success becomes the sustaining power that has kept them at Kelsey for twenty, thirty, or forty years.

A vivid description of what happens to students as they attend Kelsey came from Ryan Colter, the school custodian. "I see kids come in like this [*Assumes a slumped position, with his head down and shoulders curled forward*]. After they have been here a while they look like this [*Pulls his body up to a straight position*]—they begin to blossom."

Veteran math department head Patrick Steel echoed Ryan's sentiment: "Just the fact that you take a kid when you see them come in and their head's drooping and they've obviously had a miserable time, and they walk out a couple of years later, you know, different . . . different people. And to think that you had a part in that is . . . it's awesome."

Bert Stack noted his sense of fulfillment over the years as he has watched students learn to read:

> I think that's what people who stay here a long time get, is the sense that, yeah, you're really doing something worthwhile by being here. . . . You know that those lives have changed. . . . If they'd stayed in another setting, they would have been in bad shape and instead now, they can read[;] . . . you see transformations here. You definitely see lives changed. I know that sounds so cliché, but it's . . . I absolutely believe that; I mean, where else could you come to work every day and you see kids who come in who can't read, they literally cannot read, and they're in despair over that, whether it's outward despair or whether they come in, you know, just feeling like . . . "I'm stupid" or "I was in the wrong place in regular school"? But they come in here and that changes, . . . sometimes from the first day they walk in, or sometimes it's many years in the making. Those are probably the most rewarding.

The staff's commitment to the mission of the school and their joy in working at Kelsey is not lost on the parents, who understand the dedication of the Kelsey staff. As one parent, Donna, described it, "No amount of money could ever equate to what it's [Kelsey] done for my kids. [*Gets emotional*] . . . It's the people and the program[;] . . . they're totally different people than you come across in public school. They're just special people. They kind of think the same way I'm thinking about my kids."

The Kelsey staff's commitment to ensuring that each child finds the avenue that leads to the gateway to reading aligns with the school's mission statement. The teachers share common values. They understand the struggles the students have endured in their previous school placements, and they share a commitment to finding the best teaching tool to unlock each student's learning potential.

Kelsey appears exceptional in its mission-driven culture. Given the testimonials of some staff members, along with the documented success of the students in this book, Kelsey seems to have remained true to its mission statement.

Chapter Six

The People Method

Bert Stack coined the term "the people method" to explain how Kelsey maintains many of its cornerstone programs, such as one-to-one recitations, student advisors, small class size, and the staff training program. Bert suggested that the structure at Kelsey creates a unique educational environment:

> We live in a dream world, educationally. I mean, look at the people here. . . .
> When [outsiders] come on professional visits and they say, "Well, it's great!
> What's your model? How do you make it work? What method are you using?
> Are you using Wilson?" I always say, "No, I'm using the people method.". . .
> You've got so many people, and if they're the right people, it's going to work.
> That's the key. . . . We have the luxury of having people who are willing to
> work for less because of whatever their situation is, and that allows us to
> employ more of them. . . . We have the one-to-one [recitation class]. . . . I think
> individual attention is absolutely the key to Kelsey, and every time the econo-
> my gets like it is now, that's what the discussions are at the highest level: Can
> we do away with the daily one-to-one? What can we do? What's the . . .
> sustainability issue for Kelsey? If we stop the individualization, we won't be
> Kelsey anymore.

Bert explained that although many other reading programs exist, he believes that Kelsey's success can be attributed to the individualized one-to-one recitation approach. The people method allows for additional programming such as the student advisor's role, small class size, and an extensive administrative support structure.

RECITATION

Kelsey personalizes each child's learning program through the use of one-to-one recitation, in which an educational program evolves around the child's learning issues, both academic and emotional. Some of the unique aspects of this program include the individualized curriculum, which is thoughtfully designed, monitored, and assessed throughout the year; the intimate relationship that develops between the student and the teacher; and the focused atmosphere provided by this learning environment.

A prescribed system of assessment is used to develop the individualized curriculum. As Patty Ryer explained,

> [At] the beginning of the year every recitation teacher is given a packet for each student, and it has the same diagnostic testing for all students. . . . When that's all done, I pass that off to the student advisor, and then the student advisor looks at that, identifies the errors and comes up with a weekly plan, and then they'll give me a plan that says, by week, what I should be working on for the whole year. . . . Then, by the first report cycle, the student advisor will come up with a skills list that will be monitored throughout the year each report time. . . . And hopefully the goal is, by the end, that you've covered all the skills in it.

Patty noted that she refers to the skill checklist at the beginning of each quarter, checking off the skills accomplished as she goes. As Patty described it, the student advisor designs the curriculum for each student and supervises the recitation teacher, conducting classroom observations and discussing the student's progress.

The frequency of supervision varies between student advisors; some meet with recitation teachers weekly, others less frequently. Similarly, student advisors vary in how frequently they observe recitation sessions. Based on the student advisor's observations, each student's program is modified throughout the year as needed.

In the small recitation cubicle, teacher and student work together side by side. The match between the recitation teacher and the student is carefully designed; as a result, the relationship becomes meaningful for both participants. For example, student advisor Erin Stout noted how changing recitation teachers benefited Frank: "Last year, he really had trouble with recitation; he did not like being just one student—he didn't like doing the reading. And this year he's made huge gains; he's with a different recitation teacher and he seems to be able to trust her, and he was working most of the time."

Mike's recitation teacher tuned in to Mike's anxiety and geared his instruction accordingly. During one recitation, when Mike groaned with frustration at his mistakes, his recitation teacher responded, "I understand you are not trying to do that [make mistakes]. That is frustrating. Are you feeling overwhelmed in the reading?"

Toward the end of this session, the recitation teacher and Mike played a game, tossing a ball back and forth while naming animals as fast as they could. When the class was over, the recitation teacher explained that the game helps with word retrieval and can also relieve stress. He noted that Mike had worked really hard in recitation and needed an enjoyable break.

Students as well as teachers noted the special learning relationship that develops between recitation teacher and student. Mike expressed his feelings about his recitation teacher:

> He's amazing. . . . When I graduate from this school, I'm going to be pretty disappointed that I won't be able to go to school with him anymore or see him. When we went to the recitation session, you get to learn about each other, what he liked, what he didn't like, and pretty much our relationship extended from there and now we're really . . . well, good. I don't know how to put it, student-teacher friends I should say, I guess. . . . I'm always excited to see him every day.

This intimate relationship builds trust and understanding between student and recitation teacher that allows students to feel safe while being pushed hard in their work, even in the anxiety-provoking area of reading. In this focused learning environment, no time is wasted. Recitation teachers encourage students with regular accolades—"Excellent job," "Nicely done," "You got it"—throughout the forty-five-minute recitation session. But they also refocus students when necessary.

Recitation teachers' voices were consistently calm, relaxed, and reassuring. For example, at the end of one recitation session, teacher Patty Ryer confronted Frank about his attitude. Keeping her voice gentle and calm, she told him: "When I ask you to do something, I would like you to just do it without complaining." Then, still speaking calmly, she concluded, "OK, that is all for this week."

In this environment, students are unable to avoid working. There are no interruptions. The time is used solely to teach the student to read, and any misdirection is confronted directly, maximizing the time spent on learning.

The contrast between the recitation session and what is possible in a typical public school is striking. Inclusion models necessitate one-to-one support in the classroom and involve numerous distractions that abound in a classroom with twenty-plus students. Pullout models pose other issues, as students working in small groups find themselves isolated and set apart from their peers.

At Kelsey, in contrast, the recitation structure is the norm. Every student has a recitation class, so no student is pulled out or otherwise seen as different. Students develop a relationship with their recitation teacher that facilitates their learning in an area—reading—that has been a source of anxiety and sometimes resistance. The recitation exemplifies the value of the people method, which gives each student the luxury of a one-to-one recitation session every day.

THE STUDENT ADVISOR

As an important aspect of the people method, Kelsey incorporates a cornerstone staff position—the student advisor. Student advisors play multiple roles: They design and supervise the recitation, manage the paperwork and other responsibilities associated with the IEP (individual education plan), function as a liaison between the school and the parents, and oversee the student's entire school experience. The student advisor's unique role in the school is one that most public schools do not have the luxury of providing.

According to academic administrator Allison Tripp, the student advisor position is "semi-administrative." Full-time student advisors have an average caseload ranging from nine to fourteen students, with a maximum of twenty-one. Part-time student advisors typically have a caseload of nine students, and those who also teach two periods typically have fourteen students.

According to student advisor Anna Brush, the student advisor's main responsibility is to analyze the results of student testing, develop a recitation curriculum, and supervise the student's recitation teacher. Allison Tripp added that student advisors meet regularly with the recitation teachers throughout the year. They help the teacher set goals for the year, guide each teacher through the testing process and, along with the teacher, figure out what resources the teacher needs to achieve the established goals.

Maggie Wright, a first-year teacher, described her experience with supervision by student advisors:

> I get observed by student advisors, who give me feedback on . . . not really my performance, so much as . . . what skills I'm working on, how to work on them better, and what skills need to come next. So I've got guidance from student advisors on all recitation students. Some student advisors show up *a lot,* some every once in a while, but . . . it also has to do with how much guidance the recitation student needs.

In addition to supervision, student advisors provide support for the recitation teachers. As Patty Ryer explained, "[The student advisors are] all very accessible. . . . If I e-mail her in the afternoon, there's always a response there the next morning, or she comes to find me. So the . . . support is there if you need it."

The student advisor performs all of the administrative duties related to the IEP, including filling out the paperwork required by the state; attending all

IEP meetings, even those that are off-site; and collecting any necessary information when a student's case is going to hearing. Because of changes in special education law, extensive documentation must be filed in order to comply with the IEP. As a result, the student advisor's position has changed since its original design by Anthony Black. For example, Sally McKay, a student advisor with more than twenty years' experience, noted that in the original design, the student advisor was the "one individual who really had a sense of the individual child." The increased paperwork and meeting attendance leaves less time to monitor each student's progress closely.

Because many Kelsey parents pursue public funding for their children's tuition, they may be required to provide evidence of the student's progress at the school. Sally McKay noted that if a child's case is going to hearing to determine eligibility for funding, a student advisor must visit all of the student's classes, whereas for other students, the student advisor might visit only the student's most challenging classes. Sally described the kind of questions she asks herself when observing a student:

> Does she integrate with her peers? Does she seem to be shy and withdrawn? Or, again, engaging? Does she volunteer information? Does she seem to be making use of whatever . . . templates being used, again, are they helpful to her? Is . . . it a system that's working, and is she internalizing it? And again, at this point, what's her output? And is she making progress?

The student advisor also may be asked to attend a hearing to report on the student's progress at Kelsey—a task that, depending on the complexity of the case, can take a substantial amount of time away from other duties.

In addition to their other responsibilities, student advisors play the vital role of liaison between the parents and the school. All parents noted the student advisor's crucial role in providing information about their child. They appreciated both hearing about issues of concern and having a designated person to contact with questions regarding their child.

Teachers described feeling a sense of relief at not having the responsibility of maintaining contact with the parent in addition to their teaching load. Maggie explained: "The student advisor does everything, which is kind of nice. . . . [I can think of a] couple instances in the last few weeks, where I'm just like, 'Oh, I'm so glad I'm a teacher, not a student advisor!' I get to say, 'This is what happened. Go deal with it.' And they go deal with it."

Maggie described a situation in which Evette's student advisor dealt with an issue involving language arts homework. The student advisor and Evette's mother worked together to come up with a solution so that Evette could manage her language arts homework in a reasonable amount of time. According to Maggie, the solution worked: Evette was getting her homework done.

Both Anna and Sally observed that parents make more demands on student advisors' time now than in previous years. They see parents wanting more and more information about their child. Although providing this information can be time consuming for the student advisors, many studies have indicated that this kind of parent involvement usually promotes the child's academic success (Davies, 2002; Kim & Hill, 2015; Mapp, 2003; Toldson & Lemmons, 2013).

Given the importance of parent involvement, both Lawrence-Lightfoot (2003) and Sarason (1996) criticize teacher education programs for not educating teachers in effective communication with parents. In fact, the fault may lie not with the teacher education institutions but with the demands of the teaching job, which do not leave the teacher enough time to fully engage the parents. As noted, the structure of most schools does not include a dedicated student advisor position, which, at Kelsey, relieves the teachers of this additional workload.

Anna Brush described the student advisor as the "go-to person," who oversees each student's entire programming, addressing both academic and emotional concerns and supporting both the student and the recitation teachers to foster the student's success. Student advisors are in constant communication with teachers, providing information they need about each student and getting feedback about students in turn. As Anna Brush described it, "I read the file, disperse any information that's necessary to the teachers for them to know about whatever disability that child has, or whatever suggestions testers have had for things that work well."

For students' emotional needs, student advisors are available both to teachers who have concerns about a student and to students who need support. For discipline issues, the student advisor is the second line of defense, after the teacher. When a teacher feels that a particular student needs more intervention, the teacher sends the student to the student advisor, who assesses the situation and assigns a consequence or, when necessary, a "goal sheet" listing three individualized goals toward which the student must work during each class.

Claire, a veteran Kelsey teacher, explained that the majority of Kelsey's students had routinely experienced failure at their previous schools. She described it this way: "Programmed into your brain, 'You can't do it. You'll never learn to read or be a writer.'" In the face of these omnipresent feelings of failure, motivation can be hard to maintain. At Kelsey, where students are expected to perform in their weakest areas, lack of motivation can contribute to the discipline issues that are brought to the student advisor's attention.

For example, Frank had difficulty completing his recitation homework. After trying various incentive programs, the student advisor set up a meeting with Frank's mother to find a solution. Frank's mother felt that Frank was overwhelmed with the amount of homework assigned, and Frank admitted that it would be easier for him to stay after school and get the homework done before going home. To address the issue, the recitation teacher agreed to cut down on homework assignments and Frank agreed to stay after school to do homework on days when his mother could pick him up.

Two veteran teachers, Claire Jenkens and Patrick Steel, talked about the role of the student advisor in dealing with discipline issues. Claire noted that student advisors help teachers deal with discipline issues before they become larger issues. Patrick uses the student advisor as a place to send a student who needs to calm down. For example, this is how he dealt with Frank, who had not done his homework:

> I was frustrated, so I said, "You've got to go talk to your student advisor and figure out a time for you to do your assignments 'cause it's not happening." 'Cause *I* was feeling frustrated, so I sent the kid out . . . 'cause I couldn't send myself out, and I didn't want to yell at Frank 'cause I like Frank, and it's like, "I'm really frustrated. Go talk to your student advisor. Figure out a time that you can do your homework, 'cause I've seen nothing."

Student advisor Kelly Dance noted that she makes an effort to form a relationship with all the students on her caseload so they don't just see her as the disciplinarian but, instead, as a resource for help or support: "I really try hard . . . at the beginning of the year, and . . . throughout the year, I try to eat lunch with the kids. Sit with them. Have conversations." Kelly noted that her goal is for students to feel comfortable coming to talk with her about anything that is going on with them, "whether it's about something that you're [the student] struggling with, or you've had success, or whatever the case may be."

The student advisor position, made possible by the people method, allows for comprehensive tracking of student progress. This includes supervising the recitation, monitoring and implementing all the demands of the IEP, and supporting both parents and teachers in their work with students.

In many schools, guidance counselors and special education teachers may serve a role similar to that of the student advisor. But with a typical caseload of more than three hundred students—compared to twenty-one students for Kelsey student advisors—it is impossible for a school guidance counselor to give all students the comprehensive attention offered by Kelsey's student advisors. And although special education teachers typically have smaller caseloads than counselors, they are responsible only for academics, not for students' social-emotional welfare.

By contrast, the student advisor role enables one person to maintain a connection with the student while monitoring both academic and social-emotional concerns. The people method allows for this vital role to exist within the school, coordinating the student's academic and social-emotional concerns with other staff members and with parents.

This position, which is nonexistent in many public schools, allows the teacher to focus on teaching while another staff person manages the multiplicity of time-consuming issues that are integral to learning, such as maintaining a relationship with parents and including them in the learning process, managing the IEP, and deciphering student's academic blocks and finding individualized solutions that work.

SMALL CLASS SIZE

The people method allows for small class size—an average of five students per class at the elementary level and six to eight in the middle school. Most teachers consider small class size desirable, and students in this book also noted how they valued the small class sizes.

In small classes, Kelsey students described feeling more comfortable and focused. As Mike put it, "Four to eight kids is amazing. Twenty-two to thirty kids is overwhelming." Frank noted that small class size made it easier to learn because "it's less people and you get more attention."

For Evette, small class size meant that she got more attention, which decreased her frustration. She explained, "I'm not as frustrated [as in public school]. And I understand more, 'cause . . . the maximum in my class is seven and so the teacher can go around to everyone. . . . [In public school] they mainstreamed me into a class with twenty-eight other students. The assistant that was supposed to help me was never there. Here, the teacher has time to help everyone."

Student advisors and teachers noted how small class size allows for flexibility in putting students with similar needs together. Frank's student advisor, Erin Stout, suggested that both small class size and ability grouping (versus age grouping) give Frank the safety and focus he needs to advance in his learning. She noted, "He was in a four-person LA [language arts] class last year with boys who really had a lot of trouble writing. There were only four of them. So they plugged away at . . . three-paragraph essays with Miss Plante last year and really got the structures down."

Even at Kelsey, a class of four students is considered small, but Erin explained that these four boys needed a teacher who could provide a very structured experience that would address their particular needs, both academic skill level and behavioral issues. She noted that, in this highly structured classroom, the boys made a marked improvement in writing that year.

Parents at Kelsey also noted the benefits of small class size for their child. Mike's mother, Evelyn, noted that her son needed the smaller setting because of his learning issues. This is one reason she envisions Mike staying at Kelsey through high school: "I don't see how Mike could interact in a larger setting. I think he misses too much because of the deficits."

With only eight students in a classroom, teachers can maximize learning time. They have fewer discipline issues and are responsible for managing fewer reports and IEPs, and they are able to see every student working and to redirect students as needed.

Patrick Steel described how he sometimes redirected students to get them back on task by asking, "Are you with me?" and then snapping his fingers twice: "Nigel, you've got to look at it." "Nigel, are you with me? It does not look that way." "What did you get? Nigel, you are drawing pictures, my friend."

Patrick frequently uses humor to get students' attention: "Ouch, ouch, look at my nose. Made you look!" He follows up with statements designed to make sure students are following him: "OK, stick it to the man, like they say in *School of Rock.* What are we doing now? Everyone point to it. Will you remember all this? No, so if you track along, you will understand better. Every one point to number twenty-two." He says to Frank: "Do you have that written down? Write that bad boy down right now."

In this classroom of eight students, Patrick is like a marathon runner, in constant motion as he moves around the room to check each student's work. With Patrick's concentrated attention, students must remain focused and working—and, in fact, his students seem to be on task 100 percent of the time. Achieving this level of attention would likely be unrealistic with a class size of twenty.

In addition to paying attention to students' focus, Patrick encourages students by offering positive comments designed to help them with their anxiety: "No fear, buddy, we can help you through it." "I want you to set this up so you are really going to do this bad boy." "Do not be afraid." "I am going to make you do the next one, which is harder, because you can do it." Although Patrick might also use many positive comments in a larger class, it is likely that he would not be able to offer so many encouraging words to each individual student throughout the period in a class of twenty.

A small class also enables the teacher to quickly check that students have written in their assignment notebooks. "I am going to give you a heads-up," Patty Ryer tells her students. "I am going to give you a random notebook check. Give me a thumbs-up when you are done, and I will check that you have written your homework correctly."

On Kelsey report cards, teachers frequently note a student's need for teacher cueing to stay on task. For example, Raya's language arts teacher wrote, "On those occasions when she is distracted by a classmate, she is able to return to her work with reminders from her teacher." In both Patty's and Patrick's classes, the teacher constantly refocuses the students and makes sure they are following the lesson.

Report cards highlight this need for many students. Between 12 and 24 percent of students with dyslexia also have attention-deficit/hyperactivity disorder (ADHD), and students with dyslexia—even if they do not have ADHD—may appear inattentive because deciphering reading requires an inordinate amount of attention (Shaywitz, 2003). Small class size makes it easier for teachers to notice students who are off task and to help refocus them.

Erin Stout noted the advantage of small class size for Frank: "I think he is really getting excellent help. He could fall through the cracks in a bigger system 'cause I don't think he rocks the boat too much. He'd be quiet, but you really have to look at his written work. I really feel like the small classes and the one-to-one here [are] helping him."

The people method allows for small class size, which students report creates an environment conducive to learning. Students' accounts of their feelings of safety, trust, and comfort in an environment that allows them to stay focused and closely directed speak volumes about the benefits of the small class size that is typical at Kelsey.

ADMINISTRATIVE SUPPORT STRUCTURE

The people method allows Kelsey to maintain an unusually large administrative team. With 150 students on campus, the school has three administrators—Bert Stack, principal; Sean Richner, dean of students; and Allison Tripp, academic administrator—along with twenty semi-administrative positions: twelve part-time student advisors (the equivalent of seven full-time positions) and eight department heads. These numbers are drastically different from those seen in many public schools.

Kelsey's department heads supervise teachers in their departments and ensure that the goals of each student are met within that department. They may also intervene if a student is struggling in a class. For example, if a student reports disliking a class, the department head will meet with the student and try to understand the concerns.

The department head's role is distinct from that of the student advisor. As Allison explained, "If a student is not making progress, they can go to the student advisor or the department head. If it is a discipline issue, they would see the student advisor. If it is confusion in a class, they would see the department head."

Kelsey staff and parents mentioned the support they feel from the administrative team. Student advisor Erin Stout noted how the administration works well as a team, with individual administrators carving out their own niche and supporting one another. Erin, who had spent some time in a public school, noted the different feeling at Kelsey: "I really feel like Bert, Sean, and Allison are a very talented administrative team, and they complement themselves really well. And I missed that when I was at Callahan High

School [local public school]; I didn't feel the administrators supported each other the way that these do."

Anna Brush noted, "If I go talk to Bert about something, he's going to listen and try to fix it." Sally McKay described the support she feels from administration: "No matter what happens, Bert, Sean, and Allison have your back[;] . . . they support you. In private, you may be reprimanded, but they would never do it publicly." And parents commented that Sean Richner was quick to deal with issues and to get back to them with any concerns.

Bert Stack attributes much of Kelsey's success to the people method because it is this method that allows for the recitation program, the student advisor role, the small class size, and the abundant administrative support. Overall, the people method appears to be a key to the development of Kelsey's unique structure.

Chapter Seven

Teachers as Learners

One factor in the Kelsey School's success is the existence of unique teacher learning opportunities for both novice and veteran staff at Kelsey. Veteran staff train and mentor novice staff and are also encouraged to continue their own growth by designing and implementing original research. Veteran teachers support novice teachers both formally, through the new-teacher training program and during supervision, and informally, functioning as a resource for newer teachers.

Kelsey's design for the success of its novice teachers starts with the hiring process. As Allison Tripp explained, Kelsey likes to hire people who are good with language. She noted, "The way we teach reading, you have to get excited that 'e-d' can have different sounds. If you cannot hear the difference nor have aptitude in that area, you will hate working here. The people who are most successful are the staff that have just started teaching, who are bright people and like language."

FORMAL TRAINING PROGRAM

Veteran teachers at Kelsey teach novice teachers through a specially designed summer training program coordinated by veteran teacher Fiona Manner. The program begins with a one-week training in the LiPS (Lindamood Phoneme Sequencing) reading program, followed by three additional days that focus on spelling, writing, and learning the general structure of recitation. After that, teachers work in the six-week summer school in the mornings and receive a two-hour training every afternoon. Fiona explained the training program:

What I did [in summer training] was either set somebody else up to come in
and present a particular topic that they might be . . . expert on, or I . . . met with
them to do just ongoing training. . . . The training covers many topics, such as
how to teach cursive, how to use the pencil grips, and how is the profile of a
Kelsey student different from an Asperger's student.

First-year teacher Maggie Wright described her experience with the summer training program. She noted both the camaraderie that developed among
the new teachers and the information she received:

We [the new teachers] all became a unit, because we got all our training
together, getting LiPS training, getting general training, learning the campus,
doing all kinds of stuff. . . . We'd get two . . . or three hours of training in the
afternoons. I couldn't *pay* for this kind of training. There is nowhere in the
world that I could pay to get this much hands-on experience combined with
training. It's . . . the best program I have ever heard of.

Maggie explained that the training included learning Kelsey's mission
and history, the school's computer system, and how to access resources and
teaching templates:

Sam [a student advisor] gave us a lecture on Topic–Focus–Details, which is
where you take a paragraph and you divide it into a topic, a focus, and then
two sets of details, and then orally present it back. . . . We had times to make
manipulatives, learned different games you can use to teach the same boring
thing over and over again and have it not be boring. Patty Ryer came and
spoke about how to organize all of your materials, because you have all these
huge resources available.

Fiona noted that veteran teachers who specialize in certain areas came to
the trainings to teach the novices the various templates used at Kelsey. For
example, Sam talked about Topic–Focus–Details, Claire described the templates used in language arts, and social studies and oral language faculty
presented their own methodology and templates.

The training program continued into the school year. Teachers typically
taught five recitations and one class, leaving one period for continued staff
training: "And if they weren't meeting with me," Fiona said, "then they were
out observing veteran faculty to pull in some strategies."

As Fiona explained, the content of the training varied from understanding
the standardized tests to choosing books to read in recitation. Additional
training might include learning behavior management techniques, learning
how to teach study skills, and understanding strategies for presenting specific
concepts. Fiona added that topics often come from teachers' requests. She
then consults the person on staff with the relevant expertise.

Along with the formal training time coordinated by Fiona, the teachers receive supervision and ongoing training from the student advisors and department heads. This becomes their main source of training in the second semester, when they add another recitation or class to fill the previous seventh-period training session.

The department heads supervise teachers and provide ongoing training throughout the year by meeting with teachers regularly and also by modeling teaching in the classroom. For example, Patty Ryer explained how she got help from math department head Patrick Steel:

> My first years it was on a weekly basis, then I would have a time set aside for my prep period to go in and plan the week and say, "This is what we're working on; the kids are having trouble with this. They're good at this, I think they're ready for this." And during that meeting, he would point me to certain worksheets or other resources, like areas in the textbook. And he would model-teach, so he'd teach me.

To provide supervision for teachers concerning recitation, student advisors usually observe recitations on an established schedule and are also available to consult with the new teachers. Many teachers mentioned how helpful the student advisors were in providing resources whenever asked.

Bert Stack explained the support that both department heads and student advisors provide for new teachers:

> If you're teaching here, you know that you can go to your department head, and you can say, "Oh, I'm having a real hard time with this grouping. A: I don't know why you put these kids together." And they'll explain it. Or, "B: I'm clicking with these three, but these two aren't[;] . . . what can you suggest?" And those people are going to give you a welter of suggestions[;] . . . you're not going to be left without suggestions, resources, lesson plans on computer. . . . The same way, with student advisors, . . . if you're a new teacher, they're going to meet with you at the beginning of the year and get you started on a program for that kid. And certainly if you need them, they're on campus, they're not in a central office somewhere. . . . [Y]ou can drop in at their desk, you can e-mail them. And if you say, "I don't know what I'm doing with this kid," you're going to get back a lot of stuff to do with that kid.

INFORMAL TRAINING

Informal training occurs as novice teachers seek out veteran staff for help as needed. For example, veteran staff may find time to answer questions and provide resources to novice teachers or may model effective teaching for them. Veteran teachers understand the importance of their role in training new teachers. For example, Claire Jenkens, head of the language arts department, explained, "Another part of my job is teacher training and working closely with the language arts teachers. We share ideas and create or refine curriculum that meets the needs of their students. New teachers require a lot of guidance."

First-year teacher Maggie Wright explained how she uses veteran staff members as a resource:

> I know I can ask Sam about paragraph organization stuff; I know to ask Karen about any LiPS questions. I know to ask Fiona about math and study skills, and whenever I have certain questions, I just go to them. And they're always right there, willing to find me resources to teach it, . . . doing half the prep work with me, and teaching me anything that I need to know.

Maggie refers to the veteran teachers as "absolute geniuses," describing them as "some of the brightest minds in education." She marvels at her opportunity to learn one-on-one from these experts: "Anybody I ask a question to, either they know the answer, or they know exactly who to send you to if they don't. And they're willing to drop everything that they're doing right then and help you with it. And it's like, 'Man! Where does that exist?'"

In addition to functioning as resources, veteran teachers model-teach for novice teachers. Fiona explained that Patrick Steel, math department head, might suggest that a novice teacher observe a veteran teacher who is teaching a similar lesson: "I'd teach it so that they could see it modeled, . . . so that they felt more comfortable when they went to do theirs."

Kelsey's extensive training program, built into the structure of the school, provides both formal and informal training while also allowing and expecting novice teachers to make mistakes and to ask questions. New teachers are given supervision, support, and numerous resources to help them develop their teaching practice.

This commitment to the novice teachers was evident in the way Bert Stack referred to the new group of teachers: "This entering class, they're great." In a sense, the new teachers are viewed as students who have arrived at Kelsey to learn. Maggie Wright reported that supervisors try to provide both positive feedback and things to work on, but always maintaining a positive tone. Making mistakes is regarded as part of the learning process. The novice teacher–veteran teacher relationship establishes a strong learning community.

LEARNING OPPORTUNITIES FOR VETERAN TEACHERS

Kelsey's veteran teachers further their own learning through exposure to current research and from their own exploration. Veteran teachers expressed a feeling of being supported in their learning while also struggling with the isolation of being pioneers.

Sally McKay, a veteran student advisor, noted how the administration supported teacher growth by providing access to current research:

> The exposure that we have to research. . . Harvard, et cetera, sharing that with us. Having speakers like Miriam Wolfe; even Jeff Prince has spoken here a couple of years ago. Again, having exposure to these credentialed individuals that you just don't get in the public domain, . . . seeing what research is going on. So, you kind of have an opportunity to pick these people's brain, as well, and at least being on the cutting edge and knowing what's happening . . . in the outside world.

Sally feels Kelsey is open to changing its program on the basis of new research. She has seen many new programs implemented in the course of her twenty-plus years at the school. She noted that staff members are also encouraged to do their own research, which can influence curriculum. And on a daily basis, she observes that teachers have flexibility in how they run their classes, which allows for experimentation and growth:

> The fact that we teach diagnostically across the curriculum and it's based on . . . the dynamic that happened in the classroom today, and you can take those teachable moments that occur with children and not worry about the fact that, again, you didn't get to page 52, and have somebody come in and say, you know, "Let's get back to this lesson plan and follow it." And I think the staff appreciate that, too.

Kelsey's veteran teachers enjoy having the autonomy to experiment and conduct research, with their teaching providing a venue for learning. This autonomy seemed to emerge from necessity in Kelsey's early years, when the school lacked veteran teachers as well as research findings on effective curriculum for this student population. Both Patrick Steel and Claire Jenkens were given license to experiment and design their own curriculum based on their years of experimentation in the classroom, uncovering strategies that work with this population of students. Patrick and Claire, respectively, developed the math and language arts curricula currently used by the school.

Claire describes herself as a pioneer both in the work she has created and in her use of research findings to improve her practice. She noted that Anthony Black has been supportive of her approach, even while other colleagues preferred to use the standard curricula. In her early years, for example, she experimented with curriculum in an effort to uncover the most effective teaching methods:

> Anthony asked if I would teach a patterns class, which was Spelling Patterns. . . . [I]t was up to me to do what I wanted, so I kind of was on my own to figure that out. . . . I . . . wanted to make it appealing to the kids, but at the same time, they had to learn something. So I was allowed to do it the way I

thought was best. And I work best that way, because other traditional methods had failed these students, and I need to think out of the box.

With Anthony's support, Claire designed a writing program that is universally used throughout the school today. Along with a coworker, she published a handbook for teachers on written expression that Anthony, at the time, described as "a seminal piece of work." Claire has presented her work at many national conferences as well.

Similarly, Patrick Steel described how Kelsey gave him autonomy to develop math curriculum:

> I have such license to go and try different things. I think that's basically Bert, giving me the ability to try different things and support me when it's working out. And if it isn't, I feel like I have to change things. He knows me, so he basically leaves me alone to my own devices and he also lets me engage in all these cool things, like I can go to give in-services all over the country.

Claire and Patrick's experiences ran counter to conventional notions that teachers "learn about their own profession not by studying their own experiences but by studying the findings of those who are not themselves school-based teachers" (Cochran-Smith & Lytle, 1993, p. 1). In contrast, these two Kelsey teachers were fully supported in utilizing their own classroom experiences to inform their practice. They are also given time in their day to refine and develop curriculum. The gift of time over a longer period to do research is one factor described by Cochran-Smith and Lytle (2008) that promotes and supports the teacher as researcher.

SUMMARY OF TEACHER LEARNING OPPORTUNITIES

Kelsey's structured training program runs counter to the assumptions of typical professional development programs for teachers, in which outside experts are hired to train teachers rather than relying on staff expertise (Barth, 1990; Fullan & Hargreaves, 1996; Gulamhussein, 2013; Sergiovanni, 1994). At Kelsey, by contrast, staff teach one another.

Novice teachers at Kelsey receive formal training from veteran staff and then seek out veteran teachers to strengthen their own self-identified areas of weakness, rather than receiving in-service training from outside experts in areas identified by administration. Veteran teachers pursue their own areas of interest through research and experimentation, thereby strengthening their practice. Both novice and veteran teachers work together in an environment that promotes individual professional growth.

Kelsey leadership gives teachers the autonomy to experiment as a way of developing their teaching practice. By encouraging and supporting teacher autonomy, the school's leadership makes it possible for teachers to grow and develop in their teaching role. The message is that the leadership has confidence in each teacher's ability to know what is best for student learning—what Lieberman and Miller (2008) have described with the term "teacher as knower" (p. 21).

The best professional development comes from teachers learning from one another. They do so when they are given opportunities to visit one another's classrooms and use what they learn to strengthen their own areas of weakness (Ayers, 2001, Gulamhussein, 2013). In contrast to the "infertile soil" described by Fullan and Hargreaves (1996), which precludes teachers from growing professionally, Kelsey provides a rich and fertile soil that promotes professional growth. Giving teachers license to experiment and learn from one another sends the message that teacher growth is valued.

Kelsey's structured learning opportunities for teachers showcase a model in which veteran and novice teachers learn together in community, supporting one another and creating a learning culture that encompasses the entire school. In this professional learning community, staff education grows in tandem with student education.

Chapter Eight

A Carefully Selected Population, a Consistent Academic Structure

Kelsey's lengthy admissions process carefully selects a specific population of students who have the necessary skills to find success in the school's environment. Over time, Kelsey staff have developed a consistent academic structure that best supports this specialized population, and Kelsey teachers have become experts in teaching this selected population, homing in on the most effective teaching strategies for these students.

Because Kelsey is a private school, its admissions staff chooses the students who attend, creating a population of students with language-based learning disabilities as well as other specific qualities in common. Once students are enrolled, a structured sorting system places individual students in classes with others who have similar learning profiles.

Admissions director Lynn Kamer explained that Kelsey admits students who fit both the academic profile and specific personality characteristics. She described the kind of student they accept: "We want kids who remain motivated even though they have had years of frustration, kids who remain in the community, that show a willingness to be part of a larger group, and then we are looking for basic character virtues around truth telling, kindness. We are looking for kind kids."

In addition to these characteristics, students must fit a specific learning profile that matches the teaching expertise of Kelsey staff. Kelsey admissions staff looks for students who have both a language-based learning disability and average to above-average reasoning and problem-solving skills. Weakness in working memory and processing speed are common in this profile; typically, these students struggle with reading and writing. Lynn described the kind of disabilities they look for as well as others that they feel Kelsey cannot address well:

> We do not turn away kids who cannot read. If cognitive ability is in the right
> place, we can take them. . . . The verbal comprehension may be lower, but they
> cannot express it well. We are always looking for expressive language issues
> because we know we can address this. The only thing in [the] language realm
> that would cause us to deny a student is if the primary issues are around
> receptive language and comprehension. We do not target comprehension as we
> do decoding and fluency.

The admissions office receives over one thousand applicants a year. They turn away those who do not fit their profile. Lynn explained that many parents who apply know that their child does not fit the profile but are desperately seeking a school that will work for their child. For the past few years, there has been a waiting list. Little financial aid is available to help offset the high tuition, which is comparable to private college tuition.

In addition to the sorting process that occurs at admissions, Kelsey also places students in classes on the basis of each student's learning profile, thereby creating smaller, more selected groups. Lynn described the advantages of this sorting. "This creates a comfort level for kids when they are in classes with students . . . [of] similar ability, and it is easier for teachers to teach to [the] same focused cluster of strengths and weaknesses."

Academic administrator Allison Tripp explained the lengthy process by which students are sorted into classes. She noted that the sorting process varies according to subject:

> The oral language class looks at students' IQ, assessing the verbal score com-
> pared to the perceptual. They look for students with similar profiles to put in
> the same class. For language arts, they look to group students who have a
> similar pace on their written output. For social studies, they group by reading
> ability and comprehension. They assess age and maturity as well. Usually
> there is no more than a two-year spread in age, but there could be three.

Allison described a long, arduous process, taking up to a full week, whereby department heads spend hours sorting students into these carefully selected groups. Depending on the profile of the students, teachers may use different teaching materials and the pace of the class may vary. Math teacher Fiona Manner described how she teaches according to the leveling of the students in her class, using different textbooks and varying her teaching approach depending on the level of the class.

Selective grouping allows teachers to direct their teaching to students' specific learning needs and, according to Lynn, also creates a more comfortable environment for the students. In fact, many students reported feeling more comfortable at Kelsey than they did at their previous school. For example, Evette stated that she was less embarrassed when standing up in front of a group at Kelsey.

DEVELOPMENT OF EXPERTISE

At Kelsey, both program design and faculty priorities are focused on meeting the needs of the school's carefully selected population. Bert Stack and the Kelsey student advisors noted that over time, as a result of this focus, Kelsey faculty members have developed expertise in serving this particular population.

Many students commented favorably on the quality of the teaching at Kelsey compared to their previous school. They noted that for the first time, they understood what was presented in class. For example, Mike's comments exemplify the way many Kelsey students experienced the difference between the way people teach at Kelsey and the way they taught at his old school:

> I mean, the way they taught everything made so much more sense. . . . They didn't just shove a textbook in front of me and say, "Learn this! And if you don't, you've failed!" We talked about it, we actually learned it instead of [just] memorizing and looking at it. It was strange, because there was a higher level of difficulty in just about all my classes [at Kelsey], but everything I was being taught made more sense, so it was easier.

Teachers consistently expressed understanding of their students as well as expertise in how to best help them deal with their learning disability. Veteran teacher Claire Jenkens described the issues common to this student population—executive function issues, slow information retrieval and processing, ADD/ADHD, and, more recently, anxiety.

All teachers at Kelsey are trained to teach reading whether they are math, science, or social studies teachers. For example, in Mike's social studies class, the teacher asked Mike to read aloud. Mike began reading and then abruptly announced, "I cannot read." The teacher responded, "Do you do the ending grid in recitation?" Mike said, "Yes." The teacher asked, "Does that help?" Mike tried again but was still stuck on a word. Then the teacher said, "I will give you the middle syllable. Does that help?" After receiving this structured help from the teacher, Mike read the word correctly.

None of the other students seemed to notice that Mike was struggling with this word. The teacher's knowledge of recitation work and techniques for teaching reading allowed him to reinforce Mike's understanding and help Mike read the word.

Kelsey's sorting process, both in admissions and at the class level, creates selected groupings that allow teachers to direct their teaching precisely to the student-specific learning profile in each class. Teachers noted that these groupings help them direct their teaching to students' particular learning needs. Although students did not specify how the class grouping affects them, they did mention their increased comfort level in being with other students with dyslexia.

It is noteworthy that the advantages and disadvantages of homogeneous versus heterogeneous grouping of students remains a controversial topic in the literature. Divisions by ability have been linked to racial segregation, with higher ability groupings being offered to Caucasian students with higher economic status. (Adodo & Agbayewa, 2011; Oakes et al., 2014) In addition, some research suggests that ability grouping affects student motivation, attitude, and self-efficacy (Ames, 1992; Bandura, 1997; Maehr & Midgley, 1996, Pritchard, 2012).

However, much of the literature focuses on a general public school population, not specifically on students with dyslexia who are attending a private school. In fact, students at Kelsey revealed that they felt more highly motivated and more confident of their own abilities than they had in their previous experiences in a heterogeneous public school. Motivational theory mentions heterogeneous grouping as only one aspect of classroom structure that can promote student motivation and self-efficacy.

At Kelsey, selective academic grouping appears to provide an atmosphere that sanctions mistakes and normalizes reading struggles, providing the necessary safeguards to allow struggling readers to succeed. Many students stated they had become more interested in school since attending Kelsey. In fact, Mike, Evette, Nancy, and Frank all commented how, at their old school, they had given up, while at Kelsey they are motivated and interested in schoolwork.

Selective grouping appears to create an environment at Kelsey that makes it easier for teachers to teach while also giving students a more comfortable place to make mistakes—surrounded by similar students. As Evette put it, "At Kelsey you are no longer singled out. Everyone has the same problem."

ACADEMIC STRUCTURE

Kelsey maintains a consistently structured academic program for each subject, as reflected in curriculum design, across the curricula, and in the classroom structure designed for this specialized population. According to Bert Stack, principal, the curricular focus in every subject is skill-based and language-based. Teachers use a consistent language approach across all disciplines, and classroom routines are uniform throughout the school.

Structure in Curriculum Design

Every aspect of Kelsey's academic structure is designed to provide remediation for students with language-based learning disabilities. The curriculum for each subject is carefully constructed using templates and specific learning strategies designed by department heads and teachers for students with dyslexia. In addition, Kelsey's program maintains more classes specific to language than most schools.

In contrast to a traditional school, in which students would take only one English-language class, Kelsey students enroll in three language classes: recitation, language arts, and oral language. According to language arts department head Claire Jenkens, the oral language class was created when staff realized that students would not make headway with written language until they made gains with oral language. The oral language class is specifically designed to meet this need.

Although recitations cater to student-specific learning needs, all are similar in many respects. The main programs used by recitations are designed to address four areas of reading: *phonemic awareness* (same/different, number, and order of sounds), *linguistic patterns* (word families), *fluency* (appropriate rate and accuracy while reading orally), and *comprehension* (vocabulary, main ideas, and details).

Programs used to address all of these areas include the following:

- *Phonemic awareness:* LiPS (Lindamood Phoneme Sequencing Program for Reading, Spelling, and Speech)
- *Linguistic patterns:* Let's Read, Merrill Linguistic Reading Program, and Read Naturally
- *Fluency:* Read Naturally, Great Leaps Reading, and Reading Fluency
- *Comprehension:* a variety of resources to focus on specific skills

Among the available resources, many recitation teachers find that the LiPS program is often the key to helping children to start learning how to read. But, as Allison Tripp explained, public schools often use programs other than LiPS because LiPS is a difficult program to implement correctly. She noted that when Kelsey began using the LiPS program, the individual student advisors all had different ideas about how to implement it. As a result, the school hired an outside expert to supervise the program. This supervisory position still exists today, held by a reading specialist who also works as a student advisor for four students.

LiPS, as Allison explained it, is a pre-phonics program, designed to train students with dyslexia to hear differences in sounds that they do not naturally hear. LiPS adds a kinesthetic component: "When students make a sound, they have to connect a colored block with that sound. They also learn to pay attention to what is going on in their mouth, categorizing each sound as a 'popper,' a 'smile,' or a 'lifter,' according to the motion they feel." The student advisor designs the specific program for each student, addressing the four areas of reading.

Oral language (OL) classes also maintain a highly structured design. For example, on Mondays, all OL teachers start their classes by having students take turns talking about their weekend. Student advisor Erin Stout explained that this practice builds community and helps with public speaking: "They [OL department heads] feel like if people get to know each other . . . on a friend level, you're more apt to have better discussions when you're talking about the academic stuff and the literature. Kids have to give presentations for public speaking, and so . . . in elementary school, they get up there and they give a weekend speech."

Developed by veteran teacher Claire Jenkens, language arts classes maintain a structured approach to teaching writing, which is now used by teachers at every grade level. In this approach, students use a template to organize their writing. Claire explained how this structure becomes internalized: "They [students] can recite the topic sentence pattern, write the pattern, and then write a topic sentence on demand. In other words, the students have internalized its structure . . . [and] the students over-learn the sentence patterns."

Patrick Steel, head of the math department, described the structured math program he designed for this population after discovering that no existing math program matched the learning needs of students with dyslexia:

> Here's this brain, and we've got to figure out how to remediate within the language sphere, but no one's ever really thought about this in terms of math. . . . This is the machine you have to deal with. . . . This is the kind of material that they can take in, and this is what they can put out. So let's design the curriculum to meet that machine. And there wasn't one out there, so . . . I had to make it up.

As Patrick explained it, a unique aspect of the math program is that the approach helps students to see the overall structure (the whole) before trying to understand the pieces (the part): "By giving them whole to part, you're giving them the overall structure, the gestalt of what you're trying to build. They put the pieces in and then that drives the language. Because they don't . . . usually have the language skills to do that without it."

In addition to the "whole to part" approach, Patrick uses gross motor activities to demonstrate math concepts. For example, he took one class outside to plot x and y coordinates on a homemade oversized graph. Students placed themselves on the "graph paper" according to the individual x and y coordinates that Patrick assigned. In another class, students stood on parallel lines.

Patrick explained why he uses these gross motor activities: "The gross motor kind of thing gives them time for the language to come. . . . So, as soon as you give them a way *to* answer, then you're trying to pull the language out of them. And then you can go toward the worksheets that everybody else uses—after they have the language—but until then, it won't stick."

The consistently structured math program allows students to go from year to year hearing the same language used to describe the same approach. Math teacher Patty Ryer noted how this helps students as they move to different teachers each year: "We use that same language across the department, so that if next year Abby Gateway gets one of my students, then that . . . foundation has already been laid and the kid'll be able to connect back to that—'Oh, I've heard that before'—using that same kind of language."

As evidenced in the recitation, oral language, language arts, and math programs, the Kelsey curriculum is carefully crafted and designed to teach to students with language-based learning disabilities. The math and writing curricula emerged from years of teacher experimentation with their practice to find the best strategies. In other areas, such as recitation, Kelsey uses research-based programs that are implemented with high levels of expertise and supervision.

Structure across the Curriculum

Every Kelsey teacher is trained in the same reading program. Once trained, teachers are required to teach recitation classes, which give them an opportunity to practice and perfect their skill in teaching the program. Public school liaison Paul Standard noted that this commonality is one aspect of the Kelsey program that helps students find success. Teachers' common knowledge creates consistency across the curriculum as all students are helped in their reading skills in the same ways in every class. In fact, teacher Maggie Wright noted that in recent feedback, the state education department observed consistency in the curriculum at every level.

These strategies are evident in all subjects, as in the earlier example of the social studies class. In Frank's science class, when a student had trouble reading a vocabulary word, the teacher said, "Let's track with your fingers." The student was then able to read the word. In the same class, the teacher handed out a quiz and offered help with reading the quiz for any student who needed it. In both social studies and science classes, vocabulary words were pronounced and defined before beginning a reading—a process similar to what happens in recitation classes.

Math teacher Fiona Manner noted her own growth in the use of language teaching strategies. She taught reading during summer school so that she could incorporate these strategies into her science and math classes. As she explained it, "I do . . . syllabication exercises with those students that need it for vocabulary that's coming up in science—you know, dot-and-grab [a reading strategy]."

Fiona went on to explain "A-to-Z" sheets—a teaching method created by the language arts department to introduce new vocabulary. Students are given the definition and syllables of each word and then are asked to alphabetize the words: "[I use] A-to-Z sheets in math, when I'm introducing new math vocabulary and within the science. They're familiar; they know how they're going to go about doing an A-to-Z sheet; it's not just . . . this teacher introduces vocabulary this way . . . or that way."

Parents and students also commented on how the consistent structure enables students to advance in their reading while clearly stating expectations. Barbara, Evette's mother, expressed a parent's perspective: "At Kelsey, *all* the teachers are trained in the different protocols and everything else, so that if they're in science class and they're having difficulty accessing some of the material—" Evette interrupted: "Use dot-and-grab, use dot-and-grab. Sound it out." Barbara continued:

> So then it's across the entire curriculum, all the teachers have that base knowledge to know when the kid is getting in trouble, what props will help that child get back into focusing and working, whereas across the public school system, because there's been so many different things out there, it's going to take a long time before they can get all the teachers up to speed in speaking . . . the same language, and I think that's the big problem with the . . . public school systems right now, is that they don't coordinate with each other.

For students, the Kelsey structure organizes their learning, making expectations clear. Evette found the predictable structure of Kelsey classes less confusing then classes in public school. She explained:

> [In public school] I was told ten to twelve sentences makes a paragraph; four to eight make a paragraph; three to four make a paragraph. And then how to do math is different every year. The teachers [at Kelsey] teach it different. The teachers have the same book, . . . like I got eight to ten words in my LA [language arts] class, and then in my recitation it's still eight to ten words in a sentence. So it's like they're connecting.

Evette noticed that all teachers at Kelsey teach writing in the same way, eliminating some of her confusion about expectations. The same sentence construction template used in every language arts class was also used in every social studies class.

Teachers' common knowledge of how to teach reading strategies helps create consistency across the curriculum, which gives Kelsey students reinforcement in developing their reading skills in all subjects. Students and parents alike notice the benefits of this daily reinforcement. With every teacher "on the same page," students are clear about expectations and do not have to understand multiple teaching strategies.

Classroom Structure

Every Kelsey teacher maintains a similar rhythm and organization in the classroom. In fact, the similarity between one class and the next can seem almost eerie. The consistent structure revolves around order, process, and routine. Math teacher and student trainer Fiona Manner explained that the consistent classroom structure helps facilitate learning for students with dyslexia:

> They just tend to need so much in terms of consistency. . . . If they're going between six different teachers and each teacher runs the routine and the structure of the class differently, it's hard for them to figure out, . . . "Oh, wait. I'm in *this* class, *this* is what that person wants, so . . ." The more consistent . . . we can be, the easier it makes [it], for the child.

Consistently in every class, the agenda is on the board when the students walk in, and homework is usually the first agenda item. Most classes start with the teacher going over the agenda and then giving out that night's homework assignment. Student advisor Erin Stout explained that in staff training, all teachers are taught to start their class with the agenda on the board and to come into the class prepared with a lesson plan. Fiona Manner explained the importance and role of the agenda:

> It just lets the kids know what's coming, what's our plan for the day, so any of those kids that have tough times with transitions, they can kind of see, like, "Oh, something's winding down." "We're going to be moving to the next . . ." And . . . for the kids that might have ADD, "OK, we're wrapping up with this note taking, so I can shift focus [to] something else."

Just as the agenda helps students with expectations, giving out the homework at the beginning of the period alleviates anxiety, according to both Fiona and Maggie. Fiona noted that when homework is given out at the beginning of the period, students can write the assignment down without feeling rushed. Because they already have the assignment, they feel less anxiety throughout the class. Fiona explained:

> If we didn't [assign homework] at the beginning, they'd be waiting all period: "What am I going to have for homework tonight?" Giving it to them at the beginning, . . . answering their questions and kind of putting it out there so that they know what they're doing, allows them . . . to focus on what we're doing in class.

As part of the classroom order, teachers usually ask for questions about the homework and often allow the class to do the first homework problem together. Also as part of the order, students write down their homework assignment in their assignment notebook.

Consistency is also seen in the classroom process. First, the teachers often present material in a linear fashion. For example, in starting a worksheet, the teacher walks the students through a step-by-step process for beginning their work. In the first step, the teacher passes out a highlighter to each student. Next, each student highlights the directions written at the top of the work-sheet. Then one student reads the directions aloud. Finally, the students begin the work. At each step, the teacher makes sure the students are following along. This step-by-step process appears as a typical format for teaching at Kelsey.

First-year teacher Maggie Wright spoke about how this step-by-step, systematic instruction benefits Kelsey students: "Here, it's Step A, good. Step A, Step B . . . wait, go back to Step A. Step A, Step B, to Step C. OK, go back to A. Can you get to C from here? . . . It is spiraling back."

The step-by-step process is used in all classes. In a language arts class, the teacher first had students underline key words in the prompt. Then, as a class, they followed the writing template step-by-step, developing one sentence at a time.

Similarly, in a math class, students were taught a step-by-step approach to using a textbook. First, Patty Ryer asked students to look up the Pythagorean theorem in their textbook. After a few minutes, she asked, "Are we all on the same page? Thumbs up if you got the page." In science, the teacher announced, "We are studying the nervous system," and then asked, "Where would we find the nervous system in this book?" Next she asked students where they would find information on neurons. The classes continued in this step-by-step fashion, which helps facilitate students' learning to use the textbook.

A second common classroom process is repetition. As Fiona explained, "We've just come to learn that with our students, the more repetition and review of something that they have, the more automatic it becomes, and that's what we want for them to . . . be able to pick up the routine and slide right into it."

A third consistent classroom process is the presentation of material to students. Typically, the teacher stands at the front of the room using a Smart Board or whiteboard, with students sitting in rows at their desks. Classes are typically teacher-directed, with the teacher at the front of the room giving direct instruction.

A fourth type of classroom process is seen in the way teachers deal with focus and discipline issues. Students are allowed to have manipulatives that may help them focus, such as small toys or pieces of clay or beeswax, that they can keep in their hands.

In one social studies class, the teacher read aloud while some students chose to color as they listened. In Evette's social studies class, one student's leg kept shaking, which disturbed the other students. The teacher suggested that he rub his leg, saying that this might stop the shaking. The shaking stopped for a few minutes, then started again. The student asked, "Do you have anything I could play with in my hand?" The teacher looked through his desk, found a small box, and gave it to the student. The student appeared pleased with this solution, and his leg stopped shaking.

Classroom discipline also appears to be consistent from class to class. Teachers are diligent about curtailing side conversations and distracting behaviors. For example, in one class, a student blurted out, "I have sideburns." Another responded, "I do not have sideburns." The teacher immediately wrote both students' initials on the board and said: "I am giving you both a warning. Do you know why? You are both having your own conversations." Behavioral issues in the classroom that derail the whole class are rare, and if they occur they are addressed immediately.

Along with order and process, classroom routine is the third aspect of Kelsey's consistent classroom structure. Many structured routines are seen in every classroom. First, students almost always have only one item on their desks at a time, such as a single sheet of paper or one book. Activities change multiple times during the class, and items are always put away when finished or when the teacher suggests that it is time to move to the next item on the agenda.

Whenever the teacher hands out a paper, students are asked to put their name, date, and day on the paper in the same location for every class. In most classrooms, there is a wall poster displaying a checklist—often using both words and illustrations—of items students will need to be ready for class.

Another structural aspect of the classroom routine is that classes tend to do many brief activities. A forty-five-minute class might include as many as four activities. When I asked Patty Ryer, a fourth-year teacher, about this routine, she explained that brief activities help students with attentional issues maintain their focus—another example of how Kelsey designs its curriculum around the needs of its students.

Patty explained:

> I feel a lot of our students have short attention spans . . . and they get bored! And there's a lot to get through. . . . Frank's a great example: He's worked hard as a seventh grader, [but] he's reading at a third-grade level. We have a *lot* that we have to cover, and he *does* have a short attention span, so it helps to just keep things lively [by] moving, moving, moving through everything.

To maintain this highly consistent classroom structure, teachers must remain organized at all times. Maggie Wright described how she learned the importance of organization and consistent structure through training and from her first months of teaching: "You have to . . . be organized enough . . . so that nothing changes from day to day for them. Because as soon as there's a change, that's something that they're taking in and having to deal with, and they're not focusing on what you want them to focus on."

As an example of the need for organization and structure, Maggie told a story about what happened when she made a small change in routine—assigning two single-sided pages of homework, rather than one double-sided page as she usually did:

> It took fifteen minutes to get the anxiety down to the point where they could look through the package to understand what was being asked of them. I had one kid just . . . ready to cry, because he didn't understand how much home-work he was supposed to do tonight. One homework is two pages. Couldn't figure that out. He was like, "So I do one page?"
> "No, you do one *homework,* which is two pages." "But . . . wait, *how* many pages do I have to do? That's more homework than normal."
> "No, it's *not* more homework than normal; it's the same amount of homework on two pieces of paper."
> "But . . . then what do I do tomorrow night?"
> I had to go through the whole thing over and over again, because just that *one* simple change in format, and poof! Total anxiety.

The structured classroom environment is often noted on students' report cards, at IEP meetings, and by parents as a key element in helping students succeed at Kelsey. For example, Raya's social studies teacher wrote, "Raya benefited from a structured classroom setting where information was de-livered at a pace which she could process and where the instructor could monitor her attention."

At Raya's IEP meeting, several teachers commented on how well Raya responded to structure. The math teacher said, "With structure she can do problems and be very successful. . . . The more concrete[ly] I present it, the more she understands it." The language arts teacher spoke even more force-fully: "Raya craves structure. When there is a sentence structure she does really well."

Parents also notice how the structured environment helps their child. Lib-by, Nancy's mother, explained that Kelsey's many routines help Nancy stay on track: "I think they just keep on them, and that . . . you know, making sure by the end of the class that they know they have this homework and what has to be done, and 'Put it in your backpack.' And I think . . . she needs a routine."

The Kelsey School maintains an academic structure that caters to its specialized population. This structure, which spans all subjects, is based on a consistent curriculum design and creates a regular classroom practice that is used throughout the school. Public school liaison Paul Standard attributes much of the student success at Kelsey to this consistently structured environment. It is a foundation that goes back to the inception of the school, when Kelsey's founder, Anthony Black, described this consistent structure as a necessity for students with dyslexia.

Chapter Nine

Communication at Kelsey

The Kelsey School's structured communication system for teachers, students, and parents is another aspect of the highly structured programming that contributes to student success. For teachers, a key aspect of this system is the daily thirty-minute teacher meeting called "Snack Time," which provides an opportunity for communication that helps promote a collaborative teaching culture—something that educational reformers tout as crucial to boosting student achievement (Ronfeldt, et al. 2015).

For students, "community meeting," from 7:45 to 8:00 a.m. every day, gives them the information they need to construct their day. For parents, the key to consistent and reliable communication between home and school is the student advisor, who serves as their principal contact with the school.

SNACK TIME

In many schools, teachers cite a lack of meeting opportunities as a barrier to staff collaboration and communication. At Kelsey, Snack Time, a thirty-minute school-wide break in the morning schedule, addresses this common issue. For students, Snack Time resembles the traditional recess time. For staff, this break allows for staff and student celebrations, continuous teacher learning, and teacher collaboration. Structuring Snack Time into the daily schedule ensures that teachers have meeting opportunities every day, except for the one day each week when the teachers rotate supervision of the students' Snack Time.

During Snack Time, a staff member might celebrate a student or a fellow staff member. For example, at one Snack Time, principal Bert Stack noted that wristbands were given out to a number of students for self-advocacy and determination. Noting that it can be hard to come up with appropriate ways to recognize these qualities, he explained that the awards were given to a class that got approval from the Department of Education for designing their own testing template. During another Snack Time, Bert congratulated the track team for doing well against five other schools, noting, "It was great to see everyone participate."

Snack Time is also a place when Bert acknowledges teachers' work in putting together Kelsey's annual Community Day—a day filled with workshops presented by students, staff, and parents on a wide range of topics, "It takes a village to pull off an event like that," Bert told the staff. "It is a great tradition. I am in awe of the day." A teacher celebrated students' donation of time and energy for a knitting project: "The students worked really hard at home and at school. I showed them how to knit and then they went on their own. They made afghans for babies in Afghanistan."

Another teacher announced that he wanted to acknowledge an individual student who had risen to a challenge and succeeded: "It was just great to see him making progress." A student advisor celebrated the work of multiple teachers in helping a child improve academically: "I was at Bill's IEP [individual education plan] meeting. Kudos to everyone who worked with him. He was amazing in his IEP meeting, advocating for himself and expressing his desires for next year."

At Snack Time, it is also common for staff members to celebrate former students who have returned to general education classes, found success in the workplace, or gained admission to college or to another private school. Celebrations are usually connected to the school, but staff members' personal accomplishments—such as participation in a marathon—are occasionally shared as well.

Snack Time also provides structured time for ongoing teacher learning. For example, staff members may present a mini-lesson to their peers or may share reflections on their practice. Over two Snack Times, the director of counseling presented information on childhood anxiety. In the first meeting, she provided specific information, such as signs and symptoms of anxiety. In the second session, she facilitated a question-and-answer time on the topic.

Other Snack Time topics that teachers present to one another include lessons on computer technology, research on reading, teaching reading strategies, reading student testing, and understanding executive function disorder.

By utilizing staff members to present to their peers on various topics, Kelsey administration acknowledge and promote the expertise of its staff. Snack Time also provides an opportunity for teachers to share information about their practice. At one Snack Time, a teacher presented student posters from a science project. At another, a teacher explained a particular technique she was using successfully in recitation to encourage students to perform at their best ability. In other cases, a teacher's practice may be demonstrated by a student presentation, as when members of an oral language class performed a poem at the beginning of Snack Time.

By using staff expertise to provide opportunities for ongoing learning, the administration sends a message that they have confidence in the staff's competence. This runs counter to the typical scenario in many schools, where the administration hires outside "experts," prompting the staff to question their own level of expertise.

Meeting also provides an opportunity for teachers to ask for help in their practice, engage in professional dialogue, and share in the teaching of all students. At one Snack Time, a teacher expressed concern about a student who did not use his assignment notebook. Another teacher offered a suggestion: She noted that she had witnessed a colleague writing a note in a student's assignment notebook. The note said, "If you read this note you do not have to do your homework." This simple technique seemed to solve the problem.

Snack Time also gives teachers an opportunity to participate in professional dialogue in small-group meetings. If teachers want to talk about an individual student, the student advisor will typically arrange a meeting for all teachers who work with that student. For these teachers, the small-group meeting replaces the all-staff Snack Time meeting that day. The ease of scheduling small-group meetings gives teachers the flexibility to get together within a day's notice if needed.

At times, these small-group meetings include the student and/or the child's parents. In other cases, they are limited to staff members, providing a time for professional dialogue and brainstorming to identify the best strategies for promoting a child's success. These opportunities to meet and talk about students are the norm at Kelsey.

Snack Time offers a venue in which all teachers can become invested in every child's welfare, as teachers are kept informed about all students, not just those they teach. During one Snack Time, a student advisor asked for help from the community for one of her students: "Bobbie is having a rough afternoon. He is feeling a lot of pressure on himself to get things right. He is becoming more emotional. Please keep an eye on him. Please let me know if you see anything."

Often, student advisors will announce that a student is out sick, a family pet died, or a grandparent is ill—ways of letting the school community share in caring for the child. At one Snack Time, a student advisor noted one student's successes and another's struggles: "John started his goal sheet. He is excited about how well he is doing. Peter had the same goal sheet but is not doing that well. He had a hard time in science and did not understand why his behavior was inappropriate."

While most teachers are attending Snack Time, several teachers, on a rotating basis, are on recess duty. But as teacher Fiona Manner explained, teachers who are on duty during Snack Time carry clipboards so they can write down any issues that arise and can later communicate these issues to Sean Richner: "So I could say, 'Oh, this kid, this is the third day in a row that somebody's had to talk to him about such-and-such.'"

Snack Time at Kelsey provides a reliable time when all teachers are available to meet and discuss both their students and their practice. The benefits of the built-in structured communication provided by the Snack Time meeting are evident even to outside observers—for example, an advocate for Evette who noted that the daily communication on student progress helps make the Kelsey program successful.

BOARDS AND COMMUNITY MEETING

Dry-erase whiteboards strategically located in well-trafficked areas are used to communicate important events to both student and parents. The daily fifteen-minute student Community Meeting builds community and reinforces the information on the whiteboards. This simple form of communication enables students to take responsibility and maintain independence. Information on the whiteboards might include an upcoming dance, a parent-teacher association (PTA) meeting, or even a reminder (in icy weather) that the walkways are slippery.

Nancy's mother, Libby, explained the importance of knowing what is going on: "You [parents] always know what's going on and what's coming up. And she [Nancy] knows, too, and they put it right on the board as you're dropping them off. . . . She always knows when there's a half day; she knows when it's jean day. She knows there's a play coming up."

In addition to the whiteboards, students learn about school events through Community Meeting. As Bert Stack explains it, Community Meeting is designed to promote community and communication:

> It's a natural way to bring the student body together before they head off for the day, so that all the constituencies—visually acknowledge each other before they are divided into so many smaller groups. . . . It's also a time to make whole-school announcements about signups for sports, activities, dances, new library arrivals, news of one kind or another, reminders about policies. Finally, it's a time where special presentations happen: student council presentations, book reviews, wristbands, etc.

During Community Meeting, Sean Richner presents information students need for the day and sometimes for the next few days. Teacher absences are noted and ski trips announced. Half days and schedule changes are discussed a few days in advance. Sean Richner also reviews behavioral expectations for all students. In doing this, he takes a respectful tone, repeatedly using the word "please": "Meeting time, meeting time, please. Hats off today, please. No talking to neighbors, please. You are responsible for all the information. Please listen."

This structured communication system allows students to obtain the information they need to conduct their day independently. They are reminded what day it is, which teachers are absent, and what the behavioral expectations are. The structure gives students the message that they are capable and responsible. Community Meeting, a time when all Kelsey students are together, gives students a sense of connection and belonging that helps build community.

THE STUDENT ADVISOR SYSTEM

Kelsey's institutionalized system facilitates communication between parents and staff. The parents represented in this book felt well informed about their child's academic and social/emotional issues. For example, Mary noted how, as a parent at Kelsey, she felt "heard" by staff and administration:

> They listen. They believe you. If you go in and say, "You know, I was wondering about this," you hear from them again. They answer you. If you send them an e-mail, they'll answer you. The student advisor thing, I think is great. It's someone who coordinates the whole thing, so you go to her and say, "I always wonder about this, how about that?"

Ella noted how the student advisor keeps the link between teacher and parent open and informative. She explained that the teachers inform the student advisor, Rhonda, and then Rhonda contacts her: "If he's [Frank] not doing something he's supposed to be doing, like his work isn't done, they let Rhonda know, and Rhonda lets *me* know[;] they don't just . . . blow it off."

Barbara, Evette's mother, also appreciated the effectiveness of Kelsey's communication system:

> They give you a lot of reports, regular reports. If there's an issue, Sally McKay [Evette's student advisor] will call. . . . They send out a lot of information either via e-mail. . . . So I think that's the key thing, is that Kelsey really does well with communicating, not only with the student but with the parents, to make sure that the parents are aware of what's going on with the student.

Parents often identified ease of communication as a marked difference between their experience with Kelsey and previous experiences with the public schools. At Kelsey, parents mentioned feeling supported and informed by the student advisor's attention to their child and to themselves. In contrast, their experiences in communicating with personnel in the public school system had left them feeling disappointed and sometimes even deceived.

The importance of parent involvement has been well documented as vital to student success in school (Davies, 2002; DePlanty, Coulter-Kern, & Duchane, 2007; Epstein, 1987; Mapp, 2003, Toldson & Lemmons, 2013). For special education students, Lavoie (2008) notes that the student's success is dependent on frequent communication between the home and school. Yet, these parents recalled that when their child had been enrolled in public school, communication with school personnel often became strained.

Some parents described their frustrations, during their years in the public school system, in trying to get a true "read" on their child's academic status. Others believed that school personnel preferred not to hear from them. Libby described how the principal had interfered with her attempts to communicate with Nancy's math teacher. Mary, Ella, Debbie, and Evelyn all believed they were viewed as an unwelcome presence in the school.

With volumes of research on the importance of parent–school partnerships, it would seem logical to consider an institutionalized system to help facilitate the parent–school connection. The student advisor system in place at Kelsey provides an institutionalized way of maintaining an ongoing flow of communication between school and parents.

The same parents who felt frustrated and pushed away by the public schools found a haven in Kelsey's student advisor system. It is the student advisor position, dedicated to maintaining parent–school connection, that allows this vital partnership to flourish. Although introducing a new staff position requires increased funding, the question is this: if the home–school connection improves, will that save money in the end, with less investment of resources and time on providing support for individual children?

REPORT CARDS

Report cards serve as another means of communication, giving parents detailed information about their child's progress in school. Report cards at Kelsey are standards-based and comprehensive, identifying specific skills that the student has mastered and those that need work. The Kelsey report card has no grades; it is a booklet, approximately five pages long, which includes a narrative section. As Allison Tripp explained, the first report card, issued in October, is diagnostic, reflecting the results of testing and placement decisions made in the first six weeks of school.

This report card, tailored to each individual child's learning needs, lists the specific skills that will be taught in each subject for the year. Subsequent report cards measure how students have met their goals. For example, under the topic of spelling, Evette's report card listed thirty goals, and her recitation teacher wrote, "Evette is continuing intensive phonological training for the purpose of stabilizing firm sound–symbol relationships as they relate to decoding."

Allison Tripp noted that teachers receive training in report card writing. For example, if they comment on an issue, they must also propose a solution. "Focus" is mentioned as a common problem for many students. On the report card, teachers must explain how they are working with the student to refocus the child.

Evette's recitation teacher noted, "Evette also benefits from cues to refrain from extraneous conversation and to remain focused on the topic in an effort to accomplish the entire daily agenda." Evette's oral language teacher wrote, "In an effort to help her focus, Evette currently holds a small object in her hand (e.g., rock, play dough)." James's teacher noted, "Although James occasionally requires reminders to stay on topic, he responds well to redirection." Lack of focus is not identified as the child's fault but, instead, as a problem that the teacher needs to address. The teacher states the problem and then describes the strategies that were used to help the student find success.

The Kelsey report card contains tremendous detail about specific skills, as well as teacher comments that explain how the student's learning issues (such as focus) are addressed within the classroom. Such a report card would be daunting for a teacher with twenty or thirty students in a classroom. But for Kelsey teachers, who have only six to eight students in a classroom, preparing this detailed report card twice a year seems feasible.

Communication between staff, parents, and students lies at the heart of any successful school. Kelsey's structured systems—Snack Time, the whiteboards, Community Meeting, the student advisor system, and the detailed report card—come together in a system of communication that is viewed by parents, teachers, and students as an asset to the school's functioning.

Chapter Ten

A Supportive Community

Kelsey students, parents, and staff consistently spoke of the importance of the supportive learning environment at Kelsey in contributing to students' success. This learning environment permeated the school on every level, from administration to teachers and then to students. Four distinct aspects of the learning environment stood out:

1. Administration supported teachers and promoted collaboration.
2. Teachers worked in collaboration, encouraging and supporting one another in their practice.
3. Students felt supported by teachers.
4. Teachers adapted to children's learning issues.

ADMINISTRATION SUPPORT FOR TEACHERS

Teachers consistently mentioned that they felt supported by administration. They also noted that the administrative team modeled collaboration. This supportive/collaborative environment goes back to Kelsey's origins, but it is noteworthy that many teachers felt an increase in administrative support over time.

This support took many forms: encouraging a teacher to develop his or her teaching practice, helping a teacher deal with personal issues, counseling a teacher in his or her work with a parent, or helping a teacher deal with a student's emotional issues or academic concerns. Anyone on the administrative team might help facilitate support.

This supportive learning environment is part of the fabric of the school, according to Bert Stack. He noted that much of the support structure in place today dates back to the beginning: "I think the model that [Anthony Black] set up, the philosophy, the idea of supervisors and student advisors, the idea of . . . training, training, training . . . Snack Times, . . . that's all original to Kelsey."

Bert also noted that administration has gotten more supportive since his early days at the school and that he always felt supported by his coworkers: "Everybody here wanted to make you the best you could be at what you were doing, so . . . I always experienced supervisory support, sharing of materials, tons of training, tons of in-service."

Bert Stack, an administrator for twenty years, described his purposeful modeling of support by being available to staff and by creating an administrative structure that allows for multiple people to provide support. He tries to place people in positions of leadership based on both their skill in a specific area and on "whom other people are going to want to report to, and to have as leaders."

Bert described an administrative team consisting of an academic administrator, the training coordinator, the dean of student affairs, and department heads for every department—science, math, language arts, oral language, and social studies—for a school of 150 students. "It has to be a team," he noted. "It can't depend on one person." All these administrators are available to staff. Bert created most of these positions to increase the support opportunities for staff.

Bert noted that teachers come to him "for a welter of stuff, from personal things to students' issues to whether they're going to continue in their job at the same level or not or whether they want to try something different." He emphasized his availability to teachers, ranging from a drop-in policy to e-mail, and noted that he also makes time to meet with teachers at their request.

Administrative support may take a variety of forms. For example, Bert differentiated his support for teachers from Sean Richner's approach, noting that Sean meets with teachers specifically around student concerns. Sean makes himself available by observing students in classes at a teacher's request, meeting with teachers to discuss a student's learning profile and history at the school, and orchestrating meetings as necessary between teacher and student or groups of students. In Bert's view, Sean's availability provides "a layer of support" for teachers and staff, who know that "issues won't be left unaddressed."

Bert articulated an open-door policy that allowed teachers to access him and other administrators easily, and the teachers concurred. Student advisor Kelly Dance noted that when she goes to administrators with a concern about a student or parent, they "don't just listen to [the problem], they look for solutions." She also described how Bert "goes out of his way" to support teachers and help them find solutions, not only with work-related issues but also with personal concerns, such as a divorce:

They [the teacher] would go in and talk to him and he would be like, "Okay, so let's go to the basics: Do you have a place to stay? Do you have money for food? . . . Take as much time as you need to take care of those things, and then we'll get you back here. . . ." Those are just the things that he doesn't even think twice about.

Student advisor Sally McKay cited the supportive environment as a reason that she has remained at Kelsey for over twenty years: "No matter what happens, you know that Bert and Alison and even Sean have your back[,] . . . that they'll support you." She added, "In private, you may be reprimanded, but they would never do it publicly." Teacher Anna Brush observed, "I know if I go and talk to Bert about something, he's going to listen and try to fix it."

Teacher and student advisor Erin Stout described how she uses multiple layers of support when she has concerns about a student: "I would talk to the student's student advisor or my department head. And then, if it's sort of continuous behavioral things, you . . . go to Bert and Sean; if it's more academic, Allison and the counseling department."

Support from the administrative team was a common theme among faculty members as a reason for staying at Kelsey. For his part, Bert emphasized his commitment to creating a supportive environment based on both what initially attracted him to Kelsey and on his beliefs in a supportive administration to enhance a strong school culture.

TEACHER COLLABORATION AND MUTUAL SUPPORT

Kelsey teachers and student advisors often spoke about an omnipresent atmosphere of support and collaboration at the school. Teachers, both novice and veteran, described a collaborative teacher culture that includes the sharing of resources, lesson plans, ideas, and student homework, as well as ongoing problem solving about student behavior and student learning. Structures in place that facilitate this collaboration include a computer system that allows teachers to share files and the daily Snack Time meeting, which provides a regular opportunity to discuss student issues and teacher concerns.

Even beyond these structures, the culture of Kelsey appears to enlist teachers in supporting one another. This teacher collaboration seems to be embedded in the very fabric of the school. As Patty Ryer described it, "I love the collaboration that we have. . . . I think that one of the big strengths here is that people share a lot of materials and ideas . . . and will bend over backwards to help you."

Patty observed that student advisors go out of their way to help teachers find teaching resources without delay. As an example, she recounted how one student advisor responded immediately to her request for resources:

[The student advisor] got up, walked with me into the room, pulled down all of these different things like, "Well, you can try this one or this one or this one or this one," and popped them all next to the copier. So instead of me wading through all that, she was just [snaps finger] right there . . . ready to help. . . . That's not unusual. Everyone is like that here. If they can help, they will help.

Patty found collaboration particularly strong in her departments, science and math: "If somebody makes a homework sheet and they think it's good, they'll just Xerox it and put it in your box so that you can use it with your students. . . . I love that, I love the sense of community among the faculty and staff, it's very supportive, very strong."

First-year teacher Maggie Wright talked about the ways teachers use the computer file-sharing system to collaborate in sharing homework assignments. She described how she cuts and pastes from numerous teachers to develop her own homework assignment and noted how helpful teachers are to one another. Maggie also observed that veteran teachers help her by using a positive tone: "Here [at Kelsey], they're very positive; they're used to working with dyslexic kids. They always tell you the good stuff first; they always tell you what you're doing right, and then make suggestions that are very helpful for everything wrong."

Fiona described the comfort she felt in seeking help from fellow teachers and from administration:

I feel like I can open the door and ask Holly a question in the middle of . . . class . . . I feel like I could turn to anybody, from . . . a peer who might have that same student in their class, to the student advisors, even up to Bert. . . . I feel like I could go into his office and . . . say, you know, "I'm having trouble with *this,*" or whatever, and that . . . there's open doors everywhere and people willing to stop and listen.

As with the teachers, collaboration permeates the experience of the student advisors. Student advisor Sally McKay described how veteran staff engage in collaboration on a regular basis. She noted the ease of asking another student advisor to look over a report or comment on her writing: "We'll be drafting something and we'll [ask], 'Does this sentence sound right?' . . . I supervise Sam [veteran student advisor and teacher] for . . . another student, and . . . he'll come and say, 'What do you think about this book?' . . . No matter how many years any of us have been here, there's always something new you can learn from somebody."

According to Sally, the collaboration at Kelsey helps ensure the success of the Lindamood Phoneme Sequencing (LiPS) reading program, a complex program that demands multiple levels of support: In contrast to public school systems, where there may be no one on staff who has really mastered the LiPS program, at Kelsey she can always find someone to "bounce ideas off."

For example, Sally described the difficulty of knowing when to transition a child to the next level in the LiPS program. Because all teachers are trained in the program, there is a plethora of staff available for consultation in making this complex decision. And when a teacher has a question about LiPs, it is easy to find help. Sally explained, "If you're in the faculty lounge and they throw out, 'I have a question about such and such,' there's usually somebody there that can say, 'Oh yeah, I had that with so-and-so and this worked.'"

Student advisor Erin Stout observed, "Asking for help isn't threatening here. You're encouraged to do that as part of the culture, and it's not viewed negatively, even when you're very experienced. . . . I've been here fourteen years, and I was having behavior management problems, [so] I asked Meg [head of the oral language department] to come in, 'cause all of a sudden, you can have it down for a few years, but then feel like you're not."

Teachers at Kelsey appear to appreciate the collaboration that is part of Kelsey's school culture. They are confident they can get help when needed, and they feel encouraged to ask for help. This collaborative culture improves the quality of student learning, as teachers are able to draw on multiple resources rather than relying only on their own knowledge. Sally McKay noted that programs taught at other schools may not succeed simply because they lack the necessary support that comes from teacher collaboration: "I am concerned about a teacher, no matter how skilled, working alone in a vacuum without having others who are trained in the program to bounce ideas off of."

An additional aspect of teacher collaboration at Kelsey is the expectation that teachers share responsibility for all students. James's mother, Mia, described a conversation with a teacher who had never taught her son but still noticed and appreciated him: "Is he happy here?" this teacher asked. When Mia responded, "Yes, I think he loves it here," the teacher continued: "We love having him. He's just such a character. . . . I loved his speech for student council; I wish the teachers could vote, 'cause I would have voted for him."

Mia commented, "He's here with people who are actually looking out for him, that don't even have to *have* a vested interest in him, but do. . . . The people who work with him on a day-to-day basis really get the type of student that he is, and like him *because* of it, not *in spite of* it."

The teachers described the support they provide to one another as part of Kelsey's school culture. Novice teachers emphasized the ease with which they are able to gain support from their fellow teachers; veteran teachers spoke of their commitment to supporting and teaching the novice teachers while at the same time helping each other. All teachers noted their comfort in asking for help and the speed with which they can access that help. Teacher support and collaboration appear to be firmly embedded in this school culture.

TEACHER SUPPORT FOR STUDENTS

Kelsey teachers were able to describe specific ways in which they understood and assisted their students, and parents and students noticed this support as well. Teachers consistently showed their commitment to adapting their teaching to match the needs of the child, rather than blaming the student for his or her struggles.

In classroom observations, teachers used supportive, encouraging phrases with students: "nicely done," "way to go," "we can wait for you." When students were off-task, teachers used a gentle reminder, such as tapping on the desk or saying quietly, "You need to pay attention." In general, the teachers appeared calm and relaxed.

This may seem like an idealistic and unrealistic picture of teachers and teaching, and it is true that when teachers are being observed, they may behave differently than when they are alone with their students. But students' comments about their teachers corroborated these observations. And it is easy to imagine that managing a classroom of six to eight students would be far less stressful than attempting to remain patient and responsive while managing a class of twenty or more.

Students provided multiple examples of how they experienced support from teachers. For example, Evette described how encouragement from teachers helped build her confidence: "The teachers support you . . . and they do it with a smile on their face." She related how she was encouraged to participate in after-school sports and to run for student council, and how her recitation teacher helped her write her speech for student council. She exclaimed, "For everything, the teachers are there, they're so happy that you're doing it, and they're so really happy."

Evette's mother, Barbara, noted that the teachers seemed to have a unique understanding of Evette that allowed them to provide a deeper level of assistance: "It's like a different world, because they're attentive to her. This is how I say it: They speak her language, so that she understands what they're trying to get, and if she doesn't, she's able to ask questions more freely."

Mike observed that he could ask questions and get help from teachers whenever he needed to, something he hadn't felt able to do at his old school:

> When I have a question at the very end of school, at my old school, you'd get like, "I don't have time for this." And they walk out of the room without me even saying I have a question. Right now, I tell them, "I have a question," like, "OK," and sit down and talk about it. . . . He explains it, or she explains it all the way through until I understand it and I can do it, which is . . . a good feeling.

Teachers Maggie Wright and Patrick Steel both described how they supported students. For example, Maggie described how she addresses Raya's anxiety issues: "Her anxiety comes in when . . . she comes into, like, word problems: 'What's that? There's *so* many words on that page! I have no idea what I'm supposed to do.' She just is blinded by the anxiety." Maggie noted that by using a systematic approach, Raya is able to make sense of the information and not get overwhelmed: "If everything is in its place, there's a box for this and there's a circle for that . . . she's *great*, she's good to go."

Department head and math teacher Patrick Steel explained that he tries to create an environment that encourages students to gain confidence in their ability to solve math problems:

> I drive . . . as hard as I can, and I also send a clear message that if I didn't think they could do it, they wouldn't be in my class. I said, "You're going to make two years of growth this year; it's going to happen." And they do! It's a rare occasion when they don't make two years of growth on the Stanford [standardized test].

Patrick noted that in class he tries to focus on what students did right rather than what they got wrong. When he sees a correct answer, he asks the student to write the problem on the board. At the same time, he makes sure that those who got the problem wrong are paying attention: "So if you don't give them a way to get it wrong, but you keep . . . focusing on '*This* is right; show me how you did it,' it builds up their confidence; they're not afraid to try things. So . . . when they're wrong, you . . . find somebody that got it right and say, 'That's right, get it up there. And *you* guys, pay attention, 'cause I didn't pick you.'"

As a specific example of how he supports Frank, Patrick noted that he does not give Frank "homework makeup" (the standard consequence when homework is not done) because he wants to focus on what Frank is doing well, not on what he struggles with: "I'd rather make a big deal out of the fact that when he *does* do it [homework], it's a big deal, than to constantly downplay it, 'cause I don't see it improving. . . . He *wants* it to happen, but it doesn't happen. . . . A kid like that, do you . . . just scream at him and make him feel bad 'cause he . . . screwed up? He's already doing that himself."

Academic support was consistently available in the classroom. In Evette's social studies class, each student took a turn answering questions based on a four-paragraph reading. When one student did not get the right answer, the teacher would go back over the question until the student understood. With only six students in the class, all students can move at the same pace, with support that enables every child to gain understanding.

On report cards, teachers frequently described ways they had supported students. For example, Raya's language arts teacher noted, "Close teacher monitoring and immediate feedback on Raya's work benefits the outcome of her assignments. In order for Raya to achieve success on independent homework assignments, all tasks assigned were familiar to her because they were repeated as in-class assignments with teacher assistance before being sent home."

Mel, Raya's mother, expressed her appreciation for this type of support, noting that Raya's teachers have the "expertise" to know "what tools to give her so she can . . . move forward."

Kelsey teachers support students with positive and encouraging comments during class time. They provide individual help as needed, and the students' report cards note specific strategies teachers have used to help students find success. Students and parents alike noticed and appreciated this support.

ADAPTATION TO CHILDREN'S LEARNING ISSUES

Many teachers cited their responsibility for finding ways to teach each student that jibe with the students' disability. For example, Maggie, observing that her tendency to talk rapidly can complicate learning for children with dyslexia, explained that it was *her* responsibility to work on slowing down her language so students understood: "Jacob, I ask him a question, he responds thirty to sixty seconds after I ask the question. So if I'm going faster than that, he is just not getting it, so I have to . . . remind myself of that, and go slower."

Later Maggie described the complexity of working with students who have different learning issues even though they may be at the same ability level overall. Again, she takes responsibility for making sure that students understand the lesson:

> It's like conducting an orchestra. You always got one section that's moving a little slower than the rest, and you're trying to keep them going without motioning too quickly to everybody else, and keep everybody's attention right there. . . . They have *no* idea what we did for the period if I don't check in with them, if I don't keep the subject changing. . . . When we're switching from something as subtle as from a "why" sentence to a fact sentence, if I am not *really* slow and clear: 'OK, we are transitioning to fact sentences. What is the point of fact sentences? What is the difference between fact sentences and a "why" sentence?' If I don't do that, then they have no idea what the difference is, and it's all [just] language to them.

In one classroom observation, the teacher gave directions for a lesson the students needed to complete on the computers. As the students began the assignment, Mike appeared to be doing something else. When the teacher came over to Mike, he explained, "Oh, I didn't understand." The teacher replied: "It was probably my fault. I probably gave too much verbal direction."

Students' report cards also reflect the teacher's willingness to adapt to the child's needs. For example, Frank's social studies teacher wrote, "It is important for the teacher to check Frank's assignment notebook on a daily basis to make sure that he has recorded his assignment correctly." Rather than blaming Frank for neglecting to write down the assignment, the teacher took responsibility for checking Frank's notebook.

Frank's math teacher wrote, "Frank benefits from activities that require movement. The structure and consistency of math class has allowed Frank to make progress in math this semester." In this case, the teacher creates a structure that will help Frank find success. Similarly, on James's report card another teacher commented on the strategy she uses to refocus James: "Positive reinforcement and a sense of humor have proved to be a successful means to refocus him to the tasks at hand." Again, rather than blaming James for his struggles with focus, the teacher took responsibility for redirecting him.

In general, Kelsey teachers adapt their teaching to the needs of the student. They understand their responsibility for structuring their teaching methodology so that each student understands. If a student is not learning, the teachers look to themselves, not to the child, to make corrections. As Bert Stack explained, this is his expectation of teachers he hires:

> If your kids are doing better, as a teacher, then you're doing a good job. It isn't about how much you know, or what advanced degrees you have or your professional credentials, how well you know your subject, as much as it is, do you recognize what you have to do to communicate the information that the kids need? That's why they're here, so if they're not getting it, you've got to do it a different way, and if you don't get that, then you're probably teaching in the wrong place.

The many ways in which teachers supported their students were evident from classroom observations, from students' comments, and as recorded on report cards. Students felt their teachers' support, and their parents noticed it as well. By adapting their teaching to accommodate students' differences, teachers took responsibility for each student's ability to learn the material, rather than placing the responsibility to change solely on the student.

Kelsey's supportive learning environment operates on many levels, and this contributes to its success. Administration supports teachers, while teachers in turn support one another and the students. This kind of collaborative and supportive model decreases stress and allows learning to take place.

Chapter Eleven

Safety at Kelsey

Kelsey students and their parents alike described feeling "safe" at Kelsey. Several factors appeared to promote students' sense of safety: a forgiving, nonjudgmental classroom environment; a feeling of commonality with other students; a sense of connection and a trusting relationship with their teachers; and the encouragement they received from their teachers. Feeling safe allowed students to take academic risks, such as participating in class. All students reported an increase in their level of classroom participation when they compared Kelsey to their former school.

Department head Claire Jenkens noted the special importance of establishing a safe learning environment for students who come to Kelsey. The majority of these students have experienced failure at previous schools. As a result, they have internalized the idea that they simply "can't do it." To overcome this sense of failure, Kelsey staff provide a structured, safe learning environment, in which they demand mutual respect for all members of the community at all times and create rules for appropriate behavior. Claire describes it:

> For the new kids coming into the program, it is a culture shock. Suddenly, they're very relieved to know that they're not the only ones who learn differently. First of all, they learn that the class is a respectful and safe community where teasing and inappropriate language and behavior will not be tolerated. We have to take that programmed sense of failure away and rebuild both the social-psycho[logical] structure and the academic structure. We begin to do that from day one. We establish a community of learners and a safe environment. There are simple class rules that, if broken, will have consequences, which are thoughtfully explained.

A FORGIVING CLASSROOM ENVIRONMENT

Specific aspects of Kelsey's classroom environment help create a safe atmosphere for learning. These include the small class size and the acceptance of mistakes, both academic and structural, such as forgetting a book or an assignment. In this environment, some students felt safe enough to find humor in their dyslexia.

In the small classes at Kelsey, Mike felt that it was safe to ask questions because "no one really laughs at us." In his old school, with twenty-three students in a class, he often felt embarrassed. At Kelsey, by contrast, "Everyone [else] understands [that] you feel kind of odd and awkward [when you ask a question]." As a result of the small class size, Mike found that he was no longer embarrassed in front of his peers.

In the classroom, Kelsey teachers normalize student mistakes, thereby avoiding potentially embarrassing moments. One day in Mike's social studies class, the teacher asked students to take a sheet of paper from their notebook. When Mike looked around and noticed that his notebook was missing, the teacher simply handed him a blank sheet of paper to use. "Sorry," Mike said, lowering his head. "Not to worry," the teacher responded. "It happens. I sometimes think we should not have notebooks." By handing Mike a sheet of paper and letting him know that notebooks were not that important, the teacher attempted to relieve any sense of shame or embarrassment.

As another example, while reading a homework assignment aloud in his language arts class, Mike stopped to correct some of his writing. Then, flustered, he asked, "Can you just skip me?" The teacher responded, "We are going to wait for you. Why doesn't everyone read through their paper and make corrections?" In this way, the teacher normalized rereading and correcting, not only giving Mike the time to make corrections but also encouraging him to feel comfortable doing so.

At her old school, Evette often struggled and got embarrassed when reading in front of the whole class. At Kelsey, she found herself in a safe classroom environment in which, as she put it, "You have an option to read, and no one laughs." As a result, she often volunteered to read.

Veteran teacher Patty Ryer recalled asking her students to open their textbooks to a certain page. As one student looked through his backpack rather than opening the textbook, Patty went over to him and asked, "Everything OK over there?" The student replied, "Ms. Ryer, I brought my OL [oral language] folder instead of math." Patty responded, "No worries. When that happens, just go get it. You do not need to ask." Instead of reprimanding the student for getting the wrong folder, Patty simply gave him a way to correct the mistake.

In a few classes, students acknowledged their dyslexia publicly and sometimes with humor, suggesting that the classroom felt like a safe learning environment. In math class, for example, James started to ask a question but, before the teacher could answer, realized his mistake: "When they say what polynomial has a greater value than . . . oh, wait, I get it. Dyslexic reading problem—never mind." No one in the class said anything or even seemed to notice his comment.

In another class, when Patty Ryer announced the wrong page number in the book and then said, "You will have to excuse me today—my brain is not plugged in correctly," James again felt safe enough to add a humorous comment about his own dyslexia: "I have that all the time."

During another math class, Patty's students were playing a game involving cards with math symbols and letters. A student was unsure what one card said and questioned Patty about it: "Ms. Ryer, this is a dyslexic's nightmare—'m,' 'w,' or '3'?" Laughing, the student held up the card, and Patty laughed as well.

In still another math class, James commented to a fellow student, "Everyone makes mistakes." "Especially dyslexics," the other student responded. "Just dyslexics tend to make more mistakes," James replied. This type of banter appeared possible within a safe learning environment.

Parents also noted how the classroom atmosphere at Kelsey allowed children to make mistakes. Mel explained that when her daughter Raya started at Kelsey, she struggled to get her to go to school. As the year progressed, Raya became more willing to attend school: "It just got better and better and better as she got used to the new environment and knew that she was safe. I think that she knew that everyone was there to help her."

The value of a safe learning environment was reflected on Raya's report card as well. Her teacher wrote that Raya "has been an active participant in discussions and activities. She benefits from a classroom environment in which she feels comfortable to participate and share her thoughts and ideas."

Mike's mother, Evelyn, also noted that the environment at Kelsey allowed Mike to take academic risks without losing face:

> Kelsey has provided a safe environment for him. . . . He can take risks in this environment. And when he falls, he's not falling on his face. He might stumble, but he's not falling on his face. He's willing to read, even though his fluency is not very good[,] . . . and he knows that nobody's going to laugh at him.

The small class size, the permission to make mistakes, and the comfort in laughing about one's own dyslexia all contribute to a safe, forgiving classroom environment that promotes learning. This sense of safety helps students take risks and encourages them to participate more actively in the classroom without the fear of embarrassment.

COMMONALITY WITH OTHER STUDENTS

Kelsey students overwhelmingly spoke about the ease, comfort, and joy they felt in attending a school with others similar to themselves. The commonality they felt with other students helped create a safe learning environment. Parents, too, spoke of feeling relief that their child finally fit in. Unfortunately, in debates over the benefits of inclusion versus out-of-district special education placement, this sense of commonality is rarely identified as an important topic. Although the discourse around inclusion spans a wide range of views over many decades, it is conducted largely at the theoretical and legislative levels, with little input from students, parents, or teachers—the ones most affected by this debate.

Mike described feeling a sense of safety at Kelsey because everyone there learns in the same way. As a result, he said, "I don't feel left out, I don't feel like the only one, like I did in my old school." Likewise, James appreciated being with peers at a similar learning level: "[W]e all were, like, kind of even. So it was nice, rather than being with people who were so much better than you."

Frank observed that the students were nicer at Kelsey. When asked why, he explained, "We all have basically the same learning disability, and it's easier to get along. You know they won't bother you if you can't read something." Frank added that this was the reason he no longer got into fights with his peers, as he had at his old school: "Everyone is like the same, so it's not really . . . people yelling at you and saying you're different."

Along the same lines, Raya noted that students at Kelsey understood one another in ways that others do not: "I like that people understand what's, like, going on around them, and, it's different, sort of, like, the way our minds work; we [students with dyslexia], like, attack problems differently. And . . . it makes it a lot easier to actually, talk to somebody about something."

Parents also noted the ways in which Kelsey created a safe environment in which their child could learn. They commented that their child no longer stood out as different but, rather, resembled the norm. In addition to the academic benefits, they appreciated the social value of a peer group that fit their child, as well as the support they received from other parents in understanding the nuances of raising a child with dyslexia.

Socially, James's parents observed the ease with which students at Kelsey communicated with one another because of their commonality in learning styles. For example, they noted that Kelsey students understand one another's writing on Facebook despite spelling errors that others might not understand: "So when [James] posts something to . . . Colleen [his sister], who's away at college in Tennessee, . . . she'll say something like, 'James, what were those words? I couldn't even read it,' [and] he's like, 'Hey, I'm dyslexic. And all my friends can read it fine.'"

Mia, James's mother, anticipated that James would encounter social difficulty if he attended school with nondyslexic students: "Imagine being *the* kid in high school . . . you'd never *be* on Facebook if everyone else was spelling and couldn't read your stuff. . . . If every time you were 'tired,' you were 'tierd' or 'tried.' 'He's tierd and he's going to bed.'. . . But it makes sense to them. 'Ti-erd.'" She added, "Most of the kids [at Kelsey] . . . post videos 'cause there's no written word."

In addition to the social comfort of being surrounded by peers with a similar communication style, Mia related how good it felt to see her son as a "normal" student in the Kelsey environment compared to her experience with him in public school:

> He doesn't have to cover the fact that he learns the way he learns . . . because there are enough people here that that's normalized in his sort of realm of the universe. . . . To see him just be one of the kids, not *the* kid, not the kid in the corner, not the kid that the teachers roll their eyes at, but just one of the kids, was just so . . . *new* . . . and just . . . like, basking in this normalcy of, you know, the type of student that he was. . . . He fits in so well here.

Frank's mother, Ella, concurred with her son's need to feel like a "normal kid"—a "privilege" she equated with the feeling common to non-learning-disabled students who attend public school: "I felt if he went here, he would feel like be belonged, like a normal learning person that doesn't have dyslexia feels they belong in a regular public school system."

Raya's mother, Mel, noted that Raya fit into the Kelsey community in a way that had seemed impossible in her old school. She described how during her first year, Raya once started crying because the class was going to the library. When another child asked why she was crying, Raya replied, "Well, I can't read[;] . . . why would I want to go to the library?" As Mel recalled, "And a little boy looked at her and said, 'None of us can. What's the problem? Let's go to the library!'"

As Raya put it, "Everyone gets that we're all here for the same reason. No one makes fun of me, no one, points me out. The teachers aren't giving me different papers from everyone else. They're not giving me accommodations in front of my friends that don't need them."

Mel felt a sense of commonality and mutual support with other Kelsey parents—a feeling that they understood her daughter. She observed that parents can "tell silly stories" about their child's behavior that other Kelsey parents immediately relate to in ways she did not experience when her daughter was in public school. For example, Mel might tell another parent that Raya hates to be late, and "four of her friends' mothers will tell me the same thing."

Evette's mother, Barbara, noted that when Evette was placed in a mainstream class, she became "disheartened" about her ability rather than inspired by her mainstream peers. She expressed the view that children at Kelsey had empathy for one another because of their similar struggles in public school. Barbara suggested that less bullying occurred at Kelsey because the students understood one another.

Admissions director Lynn Kamer confirmed much of what the parents and students reported. She noted that during the admission process, "Most kids get pretty excited about coming here, thinking that they can come to a school with kids like me and look normal." Consistently, Kelsey students described feeling safer going to school with other students similar to themselves than with general education students in their previous school. They joked about their disability and relished the normalcy of their disability in this more restrictive environment.

In the Individuals with Disabilities Education Act (IDEA), the term "more restrictive environment" is defined in contrast to "least restrictive environment," and the latter is described as the preferred setting for students with disabilities. In this context, the general education environment is considered the least restrictive, while other settings outside of this are considered more restrictive.

For publicly funded students who attend Kelsey, the school is considered an out-of-district placement, whereby the child is completely removed from the regular education environment. This environment is considered more restrictive and, therefore, less preferred under IDEA, which aims to keep students integrated with their regular education peers.

The impetus for this aspect of the law originated in the 1954 U.S. Supreme Court decision in *Brown v. Board of Education*, which established the inherent inequality of separate educational institutions. The precedent established by the *Brown* ruling allowed advocates for children with disabilities to pursue the integration of special education students into general education schools, replacing the previous practice of placing these students in separate facilities (Rozalski et al., 2010; Wright & Wright, 2015).

Based on the evidence provided by the Kelsey students interviewed for this book, however, an environment that removed them from the judgment, embarrassment, and isolation they had felt in regular education classrooms and, instead, provided them with the safety and comfort of being with similar peers actually benefited these students both socially and academically.

Because their school districts tried to maintain the principle of "least restrictive environment," these students had to overcome many struggles to get to Kelsey. Although the rationale for IDEA's "least restrictive environment" requirement is a logical one for many disabled students, it also seems clear that legislators should consult directly with the students who are affected by these laws, as students themselves may reflect a different perspective on what type of educational environment is "best" for their own learning.

Nugent (2008) found similar responses in her research on children with dyslexia in Ireland, in which she compared children attending special education schools with others in a mainstream setting. Based on interviews with children and parents, she found that the children were happier in the separate special education schools, where they felt less stigmatized and more comfortable.

CONNECTIONS WITH TEACHERS

The connections formed between Kelsey students and teachers may be another factor that helps students feel safe at school. Student advisors and teachers spoke of their commitment to connecting with their students, and students and parents noticed the benefits of these efforts.

Patty Ryer, Frank's recitation teacher, described her efforts to engage and connect with Frank. She first met Frank in his first year at Kelsey, when she was his science teacher: "I tried to build a rapport with all of them, but especially with Frank because he was a very . . . tough kid, definitely had a chip on his shoulder. And bit by bit, over time, we got to have a better relationship." Patty noted how she worked with Frank throughout the year, trying to win him over. For example, she observed that whenever she gave Frank a compliment, he would typically act out the next day. One day, Patty took a chance and confronted Frank on his behavior:

> I said, "I would like to tell you that you did a really good job today, but I'm nervous to tell you that 'cause I've noticed this pattern, that if I tell you did great, then the next day, you have to prove that you're a bad-ass to me." He kind of had a smile on the corner of his mouth. So I was like, "So I'm kind of taking a chance here, but I'm going to tell you, I think you did a really good job today, and it's up to you whether you can just take that and appreciate it, and just have a good day tomorrow, or if you're going to take it and then, tomorrow, really misbehave to show me that you're a tough kid." And he kind of smiled, and . . . that was *it*, like, tough guy was *gone*.

With all her efforts to connect with Frank, Patty wanted to continue working with him the following year. She was aware of his struggles with a previous recitation teacher and felt she might be able to move him forward. She talked with Frank's student advisor, and "the stars aligned and I got him this year."

Despite her good rapport with Frank, Patty described a frustrating year trying to get him to complete his recitation homework. After employing a plethora of tricks without success, Patty finally invited Frank to order his own agenda if he completed his homework. This incentive proved successful, and Frank became more consistent in getting homework done.

Student advisor Sally McKay also highlighted the efforts to foster connections between recitation teachers and students. For example, she noted resistance from Evette in recitation when she started in the summer program. As a result, Sally described the process for choosing a fall recitation teacher for Evette: "We were very careful in terms of picking the recitation teacher, someone again that we thought that, hopefully, she'd be able to connect with." And in fact, Evette improved with the new teacher.

In general, Kelsey teachers and student advisors appear to make an effort to connect with their students. Some of the students described how they felt about this connection. For example, Mike talked about his close relationship with his recitation teacher, Peter Howe. He described their relationship as "student-teacher friends."

James contrasted the sense of safety he felt with his teachers at Kelsey to his fear of teachers at his old school. He also noted that he could joke with teachers at Kelsey in ways that he did not feel comfortable doing at his old school. While he was at his old school, he had woken up in tears from a nightmare about a teacher running toward him and screaming at him. In contrast, he recounted a more recent dream about a Kelsey teacher: "Last year I had a dream about Mr. Smith handing me my college degree, and I'm like, 'Dude! I'm thirteen!' And he's like, 'Here's your college degree.'"

James talked about how he jokes with the teachers and makes fun of them in a good-humored way. He noted that when teachers hear him imitating them, they laugh as well. James's mother also talked about the importance of the teacher-student connection for her son: "I think with James, if he's with teachers . . . who he can . . . establish a rapport and learn from, he really flourishes."

Teachers and student advisors put effort into establishing and building a close teacher-student connection, and students noticed this effort. They reported feeling a close connection with their teachers, and their parents confirmed this view. This close relationship added to the sense of safety that students reported feeling at Kelsey.

TRUST IN TEACHERS

Both students and parents described a trusting relationship with Kelsey teachers. This trust was in striking contrast to previous school experiences, where parents and students alike lost trust in teachers and eventually in the institution of schooling. At Kelsey, they were able to restore that trust.

Debbie noted this change in her son, Tim, at Kelsey. Given his trust in the teachers, she said, "Tim wants to go to school." Previously, in his old school, she had had to resort to bribing or otherwise cajoling Tim to get him to go to school. Debbie felt that he now looks forward to going to school and that his sense of trust in his teachers at Kelsey is an important factor: "The trust that he has with all the people here[,] . . . you just don't get that in public school, no matter how much you try."

Debbie also noted the trust she has in the Kelsey teachers' knowledge: "I know she [a Kelsey teacher] knows her stuff. And that's, I think, . . . something that's different. In public school, I'd say, 'Maybe she doesn't know her stuff.'" Debbie explained that Kelsey teachers try different strategies and admit when they do not know something. By contrast, she found the public school teachers more doctrinaire in their approach and unwilling to try different strategies.

Evette noted that teachers at Kelsey "stay with you till you get it." She believed that the teachers were committed to helping her, and this level of trust helped create a safe environment for learning, because she was no longer worried about a teacher yelling at her or about being lost in the class.

Ella described her trust for the teachers and her awareness that they care about Frank: "I just think all the teachers care here, 'cause they don't make much money to be here, and they're here because they want to be here. It's not just a job[;] . . . I think they really care about what happens to these kids, where a public school, I think, they just want to get through the year."

ENCOURAGEMENT FROM TEACHERS

Teacher encouragement at Kelsey appears paramount in every classroom. Math department head Patrick Steel used encouraging language in almost every sentence he spoke during his class. His most common phrase was "You can do this." Once he told a student, "I am going to make you do the next one, which is harder, because you can do it." Sometimes he said, "Yes, yes, yes," then gave the student a high five. When a student raised her hand to offer a suggestion to another student who was working at the board, Patrick said, "Give her some time, she will get it."

Encouragement in Patrick's class is not always in the form of positive words. To one student, he said, "No, I do not want it like that." Then, instead of giving up or moving on, he stayed with the student until the student understood the problem. He set parameters that students had to follow and then stayed with them to make sure they were successful.

Patrick's ongoing monologue of encouraging words was directed both to the class and to individual students. To the class as a whole, he commented, "We are cooking now," and, "Do not wimp out—you guys can do this. It will make you stronger. It is like eating spinach. It will do like it did for Popeye." To Frank, who appeared to be working slowly, Patrick said, "You are doing it. He just needs gas in the pencil."

Patrick explained how he tried to encourage students to believe they are capable: "So it's instilling that belief that 'if you try, you're going to succeed, but there's going to be a lot of failures along the way, but if you try, it's going to work out,' and it does. . . . I think the easiest way is, you show up on time, you say [*claps hands*], 'I'm ready to go, are you ready to go? Let's do this thing! No fear. This is right; show me.'"

In one class, Patty Ryer noted, "You guys are used to having a lot of success with your homework. These are hard. If you do not get them right, do not worry about it. Do not get down on yourself." Claire Jenkens encouraged a student in her language arts class with both a positive comment and a remark about something that needed work: "Your vocabulary is excellent[;] . . . you need to work on your handwriting. I know I keep telling you that. I know you are doing your best."

Recitation at Kelsey can be an intimidating environment, as there is no place for a student to hide or avoid work in this one-to-one classroom. In addition, recitation is designed to work on the student's weakest areas. But words of encouragement—"Nice," "Excellent," "Nicely done"—were consistently heard whenever a student completed an assignment. And if a student got something wrong, the teacher was quick to encourage a second try: "Let's try that again."

Mike recalled that in his social studies class, the teacher gave students the choice of taking an alternative test if the test he had given out proved "too frustrating." This teacher said, "I do want to challenge you, but I do not want to frustrate you too much. But I want you to challenge yourselves." Mike decided to take the challenge. This form of encouragement empowers students to gain ownership of their own learning.

On report cards, students are never blamed for their academic weaknesses. On Raya's report card, for example, her science/social studies teacher reported, "Although Raya has appeared overwhelmed by some new or unfamiliar activities, when given one-to-one teacher encouragement, she has responded positively." Report cards clearly state the issues of concern regarding the child and describe what the teacher has found to be helpful in addressing each issue. The student is not expected to find the solution.

Parents noted the positive encouragement from the teachers. For example, James's parents described a teacher conference that differed from their experiences in James's previous school. Instead of the litany of negative comments that had been the norm for their teacher conferences at the old school, at Kelsey they heard many examples of ways in which James had found success.

The first conference, according to James's mother, was a little "rough," as they heard about some struggles with James's classroom behavior: "He's sort of silly, he's off-topic a lot, he's, you know, he doesn't know when to stop talking in the classes." However, James's father also recalled many positive statements from this first conference, as when the teacher said, "But, you know, he's doing great. We have to pull him back, we have to redirect him all the time, but when he has been redirected, he's doing great."

In subsequent conferences, James's parents continued to hear many positive, encouraging statements. For example, James's math teacher noted, "I just want to tell you how absolutely wonderful, it's night and day, it's fantastic, he's great, he's wonderful!"

Frank's mother, Ella, described how even the baseball coach encouraged Frank. Ella cried as she recounted how supportive teachers were at Kelsey compared to those at her son's previous school:

> Mr. Cally [the gym teacher] . . . the way he coached baseball . . . whether you could hit or not, he made all those kids feel good about themselves, and I even told him that. [*Voice breaking.*] I don't find people like that[;] . . . you should feel good about yourself no matter what, and . . . in today's society, I just don't feel like teachers give the kids the encouragement to feel good about themselves. And I feel like when Frank's here, he gets that encouragement. They [his teachers] encourage him to want to be a better person, to want to learn and . . . do things. And I just don't feel like he ever got that at his old school; I just don't.

The encouragement felt by students strongly resembles the encouragement staff described giving and receiving in their own interactions with one another. Novice teachers described receiving encouragement from veteran teachers, and the veteran teachers, in turn, reported receiving encouragement from administration. When teachers are encouraging and supportive to one another, these responses become woven into the fabric of the school, creating an encouraging cultural climate. The behavior and modeling of administration and teachers reflect the ways in which teachers will behave toward the children.

When students feel safe in their school or classroom environment, they are more willing and able to participate in the lessons of the classroom (Rathyen, 2004). Reiff and Ballin (2016) noted that adult students cited feeling safe in the classroom as an important factor in their learning. The factors described in this chapter—a forgiving classroom climate, students' feelings of commonality with their peers, students' strong connections with their teachers, students' trust in their teachers, and students' sense of encouragement from their teachers—all contribute to this feeling of safety.

A CLOSE COMMUNITY

Many teachers described a strong sense of community among the teachers as a reason for staying at Kelsey. Kelsey's administrators, students, and parents, as well as the teachers, also experienced this strong sense of community.

For teachers, the strong community sense engendered a caring environment, helped teachers develop friendships, and deterred them from leaving the school. Patty Ryer described her experience of community among the staff by highlighting the support given by staff members to someone in need: "If somebody is ever struggling, everybody else kicks in to hold them up[;] . . . it's like you have a safety net under you."

Patty noted that in a year when she grappled with personal issues, she received tremendous support from both staff and administration. She received support for leaving the school whenever she needed to deal with these issues. The attitude was "Do what you need to do and we'll take care of the rest."

Fiona, who started teaching at Kelsey after graduation from college, said that she owed some of her longevity at the school to the strong sense of community. She noted what has kept her at Kelsey: "the community, the communication, the camaraderie between the faculty, and just the openness. . . . There's *so* much communication, and it's just . . . it's like another family."

Bert Stack, concurred, saying that what has kept him at Kelsey for so many years is the strong community and the collegial culture: "I always feel like coming to work and . . . this is my family, I care about everybody here."

Students and parents also commented on the strong community feeling at the school. James compared this small community with larger ones in which students tend to form groups according to interests: "Everyone [at Kelsey] knows everyone. It's such a small community[;] . . . there isn't like huge classes, like jocks hang out with jocks, musicians hang out with musicians, and smart kids hang out with smart kids, and nobodies hang out with nobodies."

The safety provided by this community of students with dyslexia allows each student to participate fully, in contrast to other settings in which feelings of discomfort may compromise students' participation and learning. This bringing together of parents, teachers, and students under the roof of one community helps support student academic success in school (Lawrence-Lightfoot, 2003). Students at Kelsey, along with their parents, all noted the comfort they experienced there, especially in comparison to their old school. In this safe environment, they participated more in class, did their homework on their own, and sometimes even found humor in their disability.

Chapter Twelve

Drawbacks and Privileges

The Kelsey School presents as a school with many strengths: The teachers support the mission and vision, the school structure allows for numerous systems that aid student success, and participants describe a safe and supportive learning environment. In addition, the students, parents, and teachers all noted positive changes in students' sense of self-esteem and self-efficacy since attending Kelsey.

All these characteristics appear to describe a near-perfect school. Like any other school, however, Kelsey has its drawbacks, as identified in interviews with students, parents, and faculty members. Some of these drawbacks reflect problems found in many schools, while others are unique to Kelsey. Some relate primarily to staff experiences and interactions; others relate to students' experiences at the school.

The topic of drawbacks at Kelsey requires some explanation. The students whose stories are included in this book all had had successful expriences at Kelsey based on both teachers' and parents' perspectives. Families who left the school and students who were struggling there were not interviewed. Therefore, this perspective is clearly biased toward those students who found success with this model and who might not be expected to identify many drawbacks.

DRAWBACKS AFFECTING TEACHERS

Unlike the common themes that emerged in the course of the interviews, the list of drawbacks found at Kelsey came largely from individual responses. These included concerns about teacher turnover rate, teacher isolation, absence of training for student advisors, lack of up-to-date research information, a privileged and embattled educational environment, and a shortage of space. Among teachers, two consistent themes emerged: low salaries and lack of constructive feedback.

Kelsey's turnover rate for young teachers has an impact on veteran teachers, who play a vital role in the training and development of novices. For example, veteran language arts teacher Claire Jenkens found the teacher turnover rate frustrating. She prides herself on the effort she pours into young teachers, only to see many of them leave after a few years: "You work hard to train them. We meet with each teacher every week to plan short- and long-term goals and to work on curriculum and classroom management. That continues the whole time that they are working here."

In an attempt to see the positive side of losing talented teachers, Claire noted that the training they receive at Kelsey will benefit other students and other school systems. However, she also lamented the time needed to train teachers and, for students, loss of the benefits of learning from more experienced teachers:

> When a teacher announces she is leaving, I have to look at it as if she is a missionary. This teacher is going to share this training in other places that could benefit from some of these strategies she learned in this program. . . . Breaking in new teachers is very time-intensive, and you know that the kids are not going to be at a pace and flow that they would be with a more experienced person.

According to principal Bert Stack, since the 1995–1996 school year, seven teachers have left each year, on average, with a low of two and a high of fourteen in a single year. The typical staff member remains at Kelsey for thirteen years, with a low figure of one year and a high of thirty-eight. Based on exit interviews, Bert noted, "Maternity and relocation are probably the two biggest [reasons that teachers leave Kelsey], followed by salary and change of career path."

Only one teacher mentioned isolation as a drawback. This was Patrick Steel, head of the math department, who talked about his experience as the only one working on a math curriculum for language-based learning-disabled students: "You find yourself on an island a lot: You're the only person saying something, and even though it's right, it can feel really lonely when you're doing that. And there's nobody else here that does math." Although Patrick sought out support at conferences and other institutions, he observed that he rarely found anyone who was working on math curriculum in the way that he does.

Anna Brush described the "learn as you go" model of training for student advisors as a drawback. She noted that although the school provides tremendous support for teacher training, there is no formal training for student advisors. Rather, as she described it, each student advisor must find his or her own style by trial and error. Despite ongoing discussions of the need for student advisor training, Anna explained, this topic gets "put on the back burner" every year.

Student advisor Erin Stout identified the limited space in the student advisors' office area as a drawback. Four student advisors share a single room, which holds their desks along with a copy machine. Erin found the lack of privacy challenging: Hearing other student advisors on the phone was distracting, and her conversations with students and parents were within earshot of all of the student advisors. Erin felt each student advisor needed his or her own space.

Patty Ryer felt that teachers at Kelsey are not held accountable for high standards, something she perceived as a weakness of the school structure. She also noted that the school could do a better job in keeping current on new research: "Staying abreast with new technology and new research[,] . . . I think we're kind of slow to go to . . . whatever the cutting-edge stuff is. And I feel like, as a school that focuses on dyslexia, we should be at the forefront. . . . If there is something that's scientifically validated, we should be doing it."

In contrast to Patty, who saw the lack of connection to new research as a weakness, both Claire Jenkens and Sally McKay took the opposite view, noting that they feel fortunate in obtaining up-to-date research information through the administration's efforts.

Approximately 50 percent of Kelsey students are publicly funded, while the rest are privately funded. Student advisor Kelly Dance described her struggles in working with students and parents from "privileged backgrounds" and her distress at witnessing the effects of an environment in which the district schools and the parents continually fight over services and money.

Kelly expressed dismay at "the sense of entitlement" she sees in many students and parents, noting, "I'd rather on a number of days work somewhere where . . . kids know what it's like to struggle . . . *really* struggle." Patty, in similar fashion, observed that she would like to be able to put her energies into the students who are not able to get to a school like Kelsey: " I think I'm supposed to be somewhere else, helping kids that aren't able to get here."

Many teachers identified Kelsey's low salaries and retention of underperforming teachers as problems. Kelly Dance noted that public school teachers earn 25 percent more than Kelsey teachers. As first-year teacher Maggie Wright put it, "The *only* thing I would complain about here is . . . the pay, that's it!" But Maggie also pointed out that Kelsey had paid for her master's degree program, and she asserted her desire to stay despite the low salary: "It's a sacrifice that, if I can make that, I'm going to . . . stay here as long as I can."

Numerous teachers also commented on the ways in which the administration at Kelsey tends to retain teachers without providing constructive feedback. Patty Ryer noted that teacher feedback becomes an issue the longer teachers stay:

> I don't think that we do a good job in giving constructive criticism and feedback to faculty and staff, that helps them to improve. The longer people are here, they grow stronger in their strengths, and more entrenched in their weaknesses . . . and therefore some problems become big, ugly problems over time, and we don't have a way of dealing with that.

Teacher Erin Stout concurred, expressing her discontent with teachers who do not uphold Kelsey's mission and vision:

> I feel like there *have* been some faculty that have . . . not necessarily . . . carried on the mission of Kelsey . . . or haven't . . . shown that they're doing their job. And I feel like Kelsey just carries them along, and doesn't . . . step in and say, "You need to change these ways or be gone."

Kelly Dance also noted the tendency to retain teachers who underperform: "We seem to be very satisfied with hanging on to, forever, . . . staff members that . . . I don't think . . . work hard enough at their jobs."

DRAWBACKS AFFECTING STUDENTS

Parents and student advisors noted drawbacks in the social environment for some Kelsey students, as well as slow academic progress and limited student engagement. Socially, the Kelsey environment can be challenging. Students must leave their hometowns and, in some cases, travel more than an hour to attend the school, which makes maintaining friendships outside of school difficult.

In addition, Kelsey's relatively small size and selected population can pose challenges for social interactions. Mentioned most by students and parents alike was the social climate for middle school girls. For example, one student advisor reported slow academic progress by one such student and homework struggles with another as the effect of social interactions.

Student advisor Anna Brush noted that Raya's social concerns interfered with her learning last year: "The social stuff had such a difficult impact on her last year, in particular, . . . it probably hindered some progress she could have made 'cause she was preoccupied with some of that other stuff going on."

Raya's mother, Mel, noted that at a small school, typical middle school girls' issues can be especially difficult because there is such a small circle of friendship:

A lot of drama with . . . girls at that age, and I think it just tripled because it's such [a] small environment; there's nowhere for them to go and to get away. And so it just keeps coming back, full circle, where maybe if it was a little bit bigger and they could have a little more breathing room, things might settle down.

Mel also noted that students at Kelsey might struggle more than students at other schools because of the social impact of their learning disability. "I'm sure Raya is like all the other girls here, that their filter system is not quite clarified. There *is* no filter a lot of times, they say things that . . . [are] inappropriate, it *is* what they really feel, but they . . . haven't quite gauged that social . . . filter yet."

Lesley, Polly's mother, acknowledged some of the struggles with the girls but reported that her daughter has made friends at Kelsey. However, because of the distance that students live from one another, getting together outside of school poses difficulties.

James commented on the difficulty he had both in leaving friends behind at his old school and in trying to make new friends at Kelsey: "I didn't make tons of friends my first year, I didn't make tons of friends my second year, I didn't make tons of friends last year." But as he talked, he did recall a few friends he had made at Kelsey, and he noted that by eighth grade he really knew most of the students in the school.

Academically not all students progress as quickly or efficiently as the staff wishes. Sally, Evette's student advisor, noted that although Evette has made some progress, she still has a long way to go. Frank's student advisor reported that Frank struggled with completing homework for the first semester of this year, although he has made progress. Evette reported that even with Kelsey's small class sizes, she is easily distracted by other students' behavior, although she added that she finds Kelsey classrooms much less distracting than her public school classrooms had been.

Some of the drawbacks reported by Kelsey staff, parents, and students represent common complaints in many schools. Other reported drawbacks appear unique to Kelsey, and some are primarily the concern of a single person.

AN ENVIRONMENT OF PRIVILEGE

Teachers, parents, and students all described some of the unique ways in which Kelsey operates as aspects of the school that help promote students' success. Many of these avenues to success are directly related to the luxury afforded by Kelsey's private school status—for example, the high teacher-student ratio and the carefully selected student population.

Because Kelsey is a private school, admissions staff are free to admit only students who meet a specific learning profile. The staff has spent almost forty years researching the best teaching methodology for this specific population of students with language-based learning disabilities. This narrow focus and commitment to research have allowed the staff to develop a consistent structure aimed at this population—a structure that permeates the school.

Kelsey teachers also enjoy a high teacher-student ratio that allows for small class size and individualized attention. The 1-to-3 teacher-student ratio that is fundamental to Kelsey's program allows multiple levels of support for teachers and students alike. The Kelsey School's mission is the common focus for all staff, providing the "glue" that binds teachers together around a common cause, building a sense of purpose and community within the staff and the school.

Although many aspects of Kelsey's model may be possible only within the structure of a small private school, public school administrators can learn some lessons from the Kelsey approach. For example, teacher collaboration is part of the fabric at Kelsey. It is woven into the ways in which teachers operate on a daily basis. Collaboration is ubiquitous, leaving teachers feeling supported by fellow teachers and administration.

Kelsey's teachers enjoy ongoing educational opportunities. The veteran teachers support and teach the novice teachers, creating an environment that allows for teachers to make mistakes, get advice, and develop their teaching practice. Veteran teachers are supported in pursuing their own research and in taking on new roles within the school. Veteran teachers also support one another, learning and growing their teaching practice together.

Kelsey's structure also provides for multiple layers of communication and support among all staff and between staff and parents. This carefully crafted communication system provides staff with opportunities to discuss student issues on a regular basis. The recitation program allows students to work on specific learning struggles in a safe, supportive environment designed for their specific learning needs. Taken together, Kelsey provides a professional learning community that has been found to promote student success in school (McLaughlin & Talbert, 2001; Ronfeldt, Farmer, McQueen, & Grissom, 2015).

These positive aspects of the Kelsey School's approach could be viewed as models for public education as well. As noted, however, the school also has its drawbacks, and it serves only a limited population. The admissions staff is able to define the student population through its criteria for admission and by maintaining the right to ask students to leave.

In addition, the focus of this book is only on students who found success at Kelsey. It does not include students who may have left the school or who did not excel there. Nevertheless, there is a need to learn as much as possible from a program that works for some, if not all, special education students.

Ample evidence for this need is seen in the ongoing problems of public school special education programs (Harry & Klingner, 2014) and in the struggles of the students described in this book and by Olson (2009) and Shaywitz (2003). Research reveals the high percentage of prison inmates with literacy issues (Grigorenko et al., 2015; Kirk & Reid, 2001; Moody et al., 2000; Snowling et al., 2000), as well as the existence of a "school to prison pipeline" (Bird & Bassin, 2015). Taking all these factors into consideration, it seems to make perfect sense to provide enough funding for public schools to implement a program similar to Kelsey's, which would provide more students with access to this type of specialized education.

Part III

The Change That Is Possible

Every Child Can Succeed

"To me, this is a really harsh reality, because wouldn't it be wonderful if all students were able to learn in their most comfortable/successful environment? For a lot of kids, they don't get this option. So while I agree that a specialized environment is usually the best choice for students with disabilities, specifically LBLD because I work with them, it saddens me to know that many other students would love to have the same opportunity, but cannot." (Kelsey teacher, January 2016)

A Kelsey teacher related her conversation with a student who reported on a student in his town. "He said, I know another girl at home who is dyslexic and they just put her in auto shop and now she has no skills, no hope of college, and no future. Her dad is a poor working-class man and her mom stays at home and picks up odd jobs when she can. They tried to fight but don't have an education and don't know how to fight or have the money. She still isn't diagnosed as dyslexic." (Kelsey teacher, June 2016)

Chapter Thirteen

A Vision for Educating All Children

The nine students described in this book, through a combination of luck and their parents' advocacy, all found their way to a school that specializes in teaching to them inclusive of their learning disabilities. These students went from feeling despair about themselves and their academic ability to finding confidence in their ability—and the satisfaction of learning to read—once they went to the Kelsey School.

The Kelsey School's structure, together with a staff who are dedicated to the mission of the school, creates a learning environment in which these students found success. At Kelsey, these students experienced an education that matched their learning needs, allowing them to progress both academically and emotionally. This was a new experience for these nine children.

From the educational journeys of the nine students in this story, three concepts emerge that may help special education directors, principals, superintendents, and policy makers shape the ways they think about "special needs" students and the structure of schools. These three concepts are as follows:

1. *Redefining access to education*
2. *Overcoming deficit thinking*
3. *Shifting traditional thinking about the ways in which schools operate*

REDEFINING ACCESS TO EDUCATION

The words *access* and *accessibility* are commonly associated with people with physical disabilities. This is what we picture when we hear about "accessible" bathrooms, buildings, or walkways. In education, *accessible* and *accessibility* are sometimes used in conjunction with assistive technology.

Access has also been defined by legislative acts and Supreme Court decisions as providing groups who have experienced discrimination with entry to opportunities that were previously denied. For example, the Americans with Disabilities Act of 1990 is designed to guarantee access to public buildings, just as the Civil Rights Act of 1964 guaranteed access to voting for African Americans.

In education, the Supreme Court's 1954 *Brown v. Board of Education* decision declared racially segregated public schools unconstitutional, and the Education for All Handicapped Children Act of 1975 (renamed the Individuals with Disabilities Education Act, or IDEA, in 2004) guarantees children with special needs access to a public education (Harry & Klingner, 2014, Wright & Wright, 2015).

However, legislative acts may give a false impression of equity. For example, Alexander (2012) notes that the disproportionate incarceration of African Americans has the effect of limiting their access to housing, voting, and employment, despite legislation that has provided such access for African Americans.

Alexander notes that the rate of incarceration of young black men in the United States is higher than for any other minority in any part of the world. And because it is legal to discriminate against felons in housing and employment, and to revoke the right to vote, she suggests, "We have not ended racial caste in America; we have merely redesigned it" (p. 2).

Similarly, for a person in a wheelchair, "access" to a restaurant might mean entering through a back entrance rather than the front door. "Access" to a theater might require a team of people to physically carry a wheelchair up a flight of stairs (personal communication, September, 28, 2015). The restaurant or theater might meet the legislative requirement of "accessibility" while not really providing suitable access to meet an individual's needs.

In education, robust research indicates that ethnic minorities and students with disabilities have been denied access to high-quality schools, teachers, and curriculum (as a result of tracking, special education assignment, and exculsionary practices such as suspension; Darling-Hammond, 1997; Harry & Klingner, 2014; Herzik, 2015; Hodson & Martinez, 2015; Lewis & Diamond, 2015; Oakes et al., 2014; Williams et al., 2015). We have not gotten rid of school segregation, mearly "redesigned" it. This segregation has denied students access to an education.

Losen and colleagues (2015) documents a discipline gap, whereby Black males with disabilities constitute 19 percent of students with disabilities but 50 percent of students in correctional institutions. He draws the connection between student suspensions and dropout rates, noting that Black males with disabilities appear to be a targeted group. If these students are pushed out of the educational system, they are not able to access it.

Inequality in education exists despite the 1954 *Brown* decision that declared "separate but equal" education to be a violation of the Fourteenth Amendment, and despite later legislation intended to improve educational opportunities for African Americans, including the Civil Rights Act of 1964. Legislation exists to specifically prohibit the assignment of lower-quality teachers to minority populations, the disproportionate assignment of minorities to special education, and the practice of disciplining students in special education even when their infraction is a manifestation of their identified disability. Nevertheless, these practices continue (Herzik, 2015; Hodson & Martinez, 2015). Inequalities in education limit access to education.

Legislative attempts to help children with learning disabilities access education were realized in part through the requirement (as part of the IDEA) for implementation of an Individualized Education Program (IEP) for identified students. For some students with learning disabilities, however, the IEP does not offer a reliable gateway to an accessible education. Questions have arisen about the testing used to place children on IEPs, the educational methodology dictated by the IEP, and the need to label a child with a disability in order to get help.

Children are often placed on an IEP after extensive testing appears to identify a specific learning disability. In some cases, however, diagnostic testing may become part of the problem rather than the solution. Researchers continually question the validity of certain intelligence tests for children from diverse cultural and linguistic backgrounds, as well as the inconsistencies in how learning disabilities are defined, which can lead to erroneous results (Büttner & Hasselhorn, 2011; Campbell-Whatley & Lyons, 2013; Harry & Klingner, 2014).

New methods of verifying a child's eligibility for special education, such as Response to Intervention (RTI), are being implemented in many schools to address the inadequacies of discrepancy testing. However, RTI also requires that a student have a diagnosis in order to be placed on an IEP (Harry & Klingner, 2014), and questions have been raised about the effectiveness of RTI as well (Balu et al., 2015).

When misdiagnosed or undiagnosed children with dyslexia struggle in school, professionals may falsely conclude that these children have low cognitive ability, are emotionally unstable, or are simply unmotivated. Students with dyslexia, even when given IEPs and other learning aids, may not be able to access the educational program that is provided, despite good intentions on the part of the professionals who work with them.

The child's statements—"I don't get it" or "I feel stupid"—or behavioral expressions of frustration may provide the most valuable information, as long as professionals can read and evaluate these signs correctly. And from the stories of these nine students, it appears that the responsibility lies with parents to read these signs and others from their children and to gain the confidence to reject professional advice and testing results as the sole measure of their child's ability to learn.

Once a child's learning issues are understood, the child needs a productive learning environment in order to fully access the education that is provided. A productive learning environment should include professionals who know how to implement the correct education program for each individual student and who understand that a child must feel safe and supported in order to be ready to learn.

Although seven students in this book were place on IEPs to customize their learning, their individual plans did not help them achieve an accessible education. But once they were placed at the Kelsey School—a school designed specifically for students with dyslexia—these students were able to access the education that was provided.

The journey of these students and families in their efforts to obtain an accessible education appeared to depend on the alignment of multiple factors, including the parents' ability to advocate, their confidence in rejecting the results of testing, their awareness of the need for a learning environment that would be tailored to their child's disability, and the relative privilege that gave them the knowledge and confidence to navigate the educational system.

Parents in this study maintained confidence in their child's ability, learned to question the authority of professionals in the school system, and became ardent advocates in their quest to find the best learning environment for their child. This often involved spending thousands of dollars on educational advocates and lawyers, as well as being lucky enough to find people to direct them to appropriate resources.

This raises questions about what happens to students whose parents, for whatever reason, cannot or do not advocate for their child. Olson (2009) quotes a college student who, reflecting back on her school experience, noted that the lack of parental advocacy "allowed the school to sweep me under the rug" (pp. 48–49). The circuitous route taken by these nine students is evidence of an inequitable process whereby some students find access while others may be denied.

Given this pathway, it is easy to imagine that many students do not find their way to an accessible education. Some children are tested and are believed to be working at their best ability, which by many measures may simply be considered low. These children may stay at this level unless their parents question the results and advocate for new testing that can reveal the existence of a learning disability that is impeding the child's educational progress.

The avenue taken may depend on the parents' degree of involvement in the school, their socioeconomic status, the attitudes of the professionals in the school system, and the quality of the testing, among other factors. For some children, emotional problems may mask a learning disability. These children may remain in a holding pattern, lacking the tools to move forward in their education, or, worse, they may become part of a discipline cycle where they are routinely pushed out of the classroom. Other children may be diagnosed and assigned a special education label when, in fact, it is a poor educational environment that is impeding their learning, not a problem with the child's learning style (Harry & Klingner, 2014; Losen et al., 2015).

In this book, each child's parent played a key role in recognizing the signs and symptoms of a child frustrated with school. The child's frustration galvanized the parents to advocate for their child's education. But access to education cannot be solely dependent on parent advocacy. Not all parents have the skills, knoweldge, social and cultural capital, time, and financial stabilty to become effective educational advocates for their children, yet every child deserves access to an appropriate education.

Access to education needs to move beyond legislative actions and directly to the students. It cannot be a privilege bestowed on some and denied to others on the basis of race, class, or socioeconomic status. Rather, access to education must mean that *every* child is given a pathway to pursue educational success.

OVERCOMING DEFICIT THINKING: CREATING A "SPECIAL EDUCATION" FOR ALL STUDENTS

Deficit thinking has too long been used to explain students' struggles in school. This kind of thinking suggests that the problems lie within the child rather than the teaching methodology. As a result, children are labeled with a disability, without any attempt to decipher each child's way of learning. Among other things, deficit thinking has been used to sanction racism and to support unwarranted assumptions about students from racial or ethnic minority groups.

Deficit thinking is used to explain student failure by blaming the student's perceived cognitive ability, lack of motivation, or family issues rather than looking within the school itself for solutions. Valencia (1997) explains that deficit thinking has been around since the 1600s and that this model is "rooted in ignorance, classism, racism, sexism, pseudoscience, and methodologically flawed research" (p. xii).

Students in this study talked about their scars from years in a school system that did not know how to teach them. They endured a system that demanded that they be given a diagnosis in order to receive an education. They were pulled out of class and labeled with a problem, but their learning needs were still not met.

From the inception of special education, its design promoted segregation and normed criteria in order to facilitate separation of identified students from the general education population. This process can harm individuals who must live with a deficit label, and it can also harm whole groups, as seen in the overrepresentation of minority students in special education.

Inequities in the identification of students for special education services, along with the consequences of segregating a group of students from the general population, suggest that special education is not always so special. Given the multitude of problems with the assignment of students to special education and the negative consequences of comparing students with an artificial norm, a move away from traditional special education programs is urgently needed.

The inclusion movement promotes differentiated instruction and universal design for learning as ways to include all students in the general education classroom. Even with this model, however, students who require "special education" are still labeled and segregated from the "norm." There is a need to alter the identification of special education and to develop a model that is truly inclusive.

With a new approach to special education, students would no longer need to face comparison to an artificial norm. Instead, every child would be viewed as unique; *difference* would become the norm (Gurn, 2010). So, for example, reading help might be available for all students who need it, not just those who meet arbitrary criteria.

Gallagher (2010) promotes the use of the term *belonging* to replace *inclusion*. She notes that "inclusion" has come to be *exclusion*, whereas the idea of belonging promotes acceptance and understanding that although everyone is different, all students belong to the larger group. With belonging as the norm, students would no longer need to meet specific criteria to get services and would no longer need to live with a feeling of deficiency. Shifting away from traditional special education might provide all students with equal access to a "special education," instead of relying on criteria that often depend on each child's school, teachers, and parents.

Sailor (2015) describes an "equity-based definition of inclusion" (p. 94). This vision provides students with the best instructional situation to meet their educational needs, rather than simply placing students in the least restrictive environmnet. In a reversal of the idea of labeling the student, this approach places students' learning differences on the context of the environment.

Edward Hallowell (personal communication, January 28, 2011) provides a framework for altering the discourse around the concept of "disability." He notes that a diagnosis of ADHD (attention-deficit/hyperactivity disorder), commonly viewed as a disability, might instead be considered normal and even highlighted as advantageous. For example, students who are more active may get more done in a day than other students.

Hallowell comments that it would be just as easy to define people with a greater degree of focus with a label like "Over Focus Disorder (OFD)," noting that the tendency to overfocus limits these individuals' ability to get more things done in a day. In other words, both groups have advantages and disadvantages, and these can be celebrated rather than being viewed as deficits.

Armstrong (2010) uses the term "neurodiversity" (p. 3) to describe neurological differences in people's brains. Like Hallowell, he notes that many advantages of commonly defined neurological disabilities, such as dyslexia, autism, and ADHD, may be overlooked in the rush to assign a pathological label to brain differences. He suggests that these differences should be understood instead as gifts, providing unique strengths from which people can learn.

Armstrong argues that along with bio-, cultural, and racial diversity, brain diversity needs to hold a place in societal discourse about differences, so that we reorient our thinking to appreciate all the naturally occurring differences in the human brain. He advocates for "a new field of neurodiversity" (p. 3), where there is no "normal" brain to which other brains are compared.

Judy Singer, a parent of a child with Asperger's syndrome, is credited with coining the term *neurodiversity* (Armstrong, 2010). Armstrong notes that the term was part of "a movement among individuals labeled with autism spectrum disorder (ASD) who wanted to be seen as different, not disabled" (p. 7). Armstrong suggests that we look for the gifts offered by each different kind of brain, rather than the deficits.

It seems to make more sense to think about every child as having a gift and to recognize that no one type of brain is the "model" brain to which we should all aspire. In fact, individual human brains differ in many significant ways, and these differences should inform the ways in which we teach.

For the students in this book, the opportunity to find their gifts, understand their talents, and know that they were just as capable as other students came only when they were able to attend a school where the norm was for children to be identified with dyslexia. This type of environment is not available to all students; yet all students may need to feel they have individual strengths and weaknesses, rather than a disability defined in relation to a mythical norm. This is the type of thinking that may move schools past the deficit model.

Much of the current discourse on inclusive educational environments focuses on students' strengths rather than their weaknesses, suggesting a potential move away from deficit thinking and labeling (Salend, 2016). Yet students are still caught in the system of labels as a way to identify challenges that may in fact be environmental, cultural, or in some other way beyond a student's control.

Ladson-Billings (2006) provides an example of how changing the terminology we use can actually change the way problems are approached. As an example, she uses the term "educational debt" (p. 6) to replace the commonly used term "achievement gap" (p. 3). She suggests that the concept of "educational debt" places issues of racism and classism at the forefront, moving the discussion to the political arena and away from blaming the child.

Moving away from the tradition of deficit thinking in special education may mean that more students will get the services they need and that teachers will get additional training so that students no longer are blamed for not grasping what is taught in class. Labeling children should not be the route by which children can qualify for services (Gold & Richards, 2012; Gurn, 2010).

SHIFTING THE WAYS IN WHICH SCHOOLS OPERATE

The teacher culture in many schools is characterized by isolation, despite evidence suggesting that a collaborative teacher culture based on the idea of a professional learning community would create a sustaining environment that would enable more students to achieve. Many schools have moved toward incorporating a collaborative culture, but rigid school structures often sabotage this effort (Fullan & Hargreaves, 1996; Ketterlin-Geller, Baumer, & Lichon, 2015; Salend, 2016; Wehlage et al., 1996).

The Kelsey School provides a model of a professional learning environment where teachers and administration practice and embrace collaboration on a daily basis and where teacher education is embedded in the school structure. This structure may serve as an example for other schools. As a private school, Kelsey enjoys certain advantages that facilitate such a culture of learning. However, a shift is possible in public schools as well.

One structural change that would promote this shift might involve adopting Bert Stack's "people method." Bert described the success of the Kelsey School on his use of this method, noting that without the efforts of the entire staff, the school would not have been able to create its distinctive instructional environment, which has enabled so many students to become successful.

Teachers are being asked to do more and more every day—to implement a myriad of new curricula as well as programs such as Response to Intervention (RTI), Universal Design for Learning (UDL), and Differentiated Instruction (DI). They are asked to create an inclusive classroom but often are not given the supports or tools they would need to accomplish this. Instead, as the Kelsey experience suggests, they may simply need "The People Method" (TPM) to be successful in teaching all students.

The typical classroom structure, with twenty or more students under the educational direction of a single teacher, does not allow for the individualized attention that many students—such as those who found their way to the Kelsey School—need to succeed. Although many of the students in this book struggled with their public school experience, parents and students alike often recognized that the teachers were not at fault but, rather, they were caught within a dysfunctional system that lacked the necessary supports.

Lack of funding is often blamed for preventing public schools from embracing the people method. Yet the federal government and individual states spend millions of dollars supporting the system of standardized testing that has failed to increase student achievement (Sahlberg, 2011; Zernike, 2016). Additionally, billions of dollars are spent annually to incarcerate youth as students continue to enter the so-called "school-to-prison pipeline" (Petteruti, Schindler, & Ziedenberg, 2014). Today's funding priorities need to be shifted.

Even if lack of funding would prevent schools from adopting the people method, a structural change such as the one used in the Finnish school system could accomplish the same goals. Sahlberg (2011) describes how the Finnish school system supports higher levels of student achievement through similar systemic changes. Rather than employing more teachers, as the people method requires, in the Finnish system, teachers do less. They teach for fewer hours than U.S. teachers, and this schedule gives them time to collaborate with other teachres. Students are assigned little or no homework, which also gives teachers more time. Finally, teachers do not have to spend valuable teaching time administering standardized tests.

A second essential structural change is the development of a strong school cutlure. For example, schools could maintain the position of "superintendent of culture" rather than the traditional "superintendent of curriculum and instruction." Some schools have instituted a "dean of culture," but often this person simply becomes a disciplinarian.

With ample evidence that a collaborative teacher culture enhances student achievement, it would make sense for top-level administration to provide both expertise and support in maintaining cultures that maximize student learning. In this approach, the head administrator would model collaboration and create a structure to allow teachers and principals time and space to work together so they can have ownership of curriculum and instruction.

Schein (2004) provides an example of leaders in an organization modeling teamwork that had an impact on the core functioning of the company. He describes the culture of Hewlett Packard (HP) as the "HP way" (p. 29). William Hewlett had a technology background, while David Packard brought business experience to the company. The HP way emphasized teamwork. The founders teamed together, using their respective areas of expertise to move the company forward. The HP way permeated all areas of the company, where teamwork became the norm.

If a school's superintendent of culture models collaborative leadership while also providing the support that principals and teachers need to maintain a collaborative teacher culture, both teachers and principals might be able to ease into this culture.

A third shift would require teachers, principals, and students to view all teachers and administrators as part of the team helping each individual child. In this culture, no single teacher is responsible for certain children's achievement. Instead, every teacher shares responsibility for every child.

This is another successful feature seen in Finnish schools (Sahlberg, 2011). Assessments are shared across classrooms, and both successes and failures are "owned" by all staff. The "Snack Time" meeting at Kelsey helped establish the shared "ownership" of all students, providing a setting in which teachers could share successes, failures, and information about specific students. During Snack Time, teachers can ask for help with ways to address a struggling student. Kelsey also uses the student advising system to facilitate teachers working together to help each child achieve to the best of his or her ability.

A fourth shift in culture requires bringing issues of trust to the forefront. More than staff parties and community-building activities such as ropes courses, discourse on trust needs to have a prominent position in schools. This entails commitment on the part of the principal and staff, as it is easier to change curriculum every year than to talk about deep trust.

Sahlberg (2011) highlights the trust that has developed within the Finnish schools. Teachers' professional knowledge is trusted, and the schools build on teacher strengths. Sahlberg describes a "trust-based school culture" (p. 130) as a key feature that has helped the reform of education in Finland.

As Meier (2002) discovered when she opened her second school, developing trust takes time as well as the structure and leadership to allow trust to develop. Trust needs to be part of the everyday language of the school. Teachers need to talk about trusting one another and making themselves vulnerable, and administrators need to trust teacher knowledge and expertise, and to give teachers freedom to make mistakes that will facilitate learning. Parents need to trust the teachers as well.

At Kelsey, strong bonds between veteran teachers and novice teachers helped establish a feeling of trust. Novice teachers were expected to make mistakes, and veteran teachers provided support and learning. Parents developed trust in Kelsey teachers when they saw their child succeeding.

In order to give teachers the time, space, and support to make learning the focus for all students, schools need to undergo structural change. As Barth (1990) explains, teachers, students, and administrators need to become messy with the "clay" of learning (p. 94). The Kelsey School provides such a model. Teachers, students, and administrators allow one another to make mistakes without judgment. There are times for self-reflection, chances to receive feedback from peers, and ownership for all students who are not labeled in a deficit manner. In this way, the school becomes a true learning organization.

With this shift, a genuinely collaborative and trusting culture emerges. It removes the barriers created by traditional school structures and, instead, exemplifies what teachers and principals can achieve when given autonomy, tools, and support to become "messy" with learning.

LESSONS LEARNED FROM KELSEY

It is beyond the scope of this book to propose a plan for educational reform. Rather, the intent is to learn from the nine students in this book and from the model of the Kelsey School that allowed these children to access an education when no other system had worked for them. It is also the intent of this book to acknowledge the inequities that exist on many levels of our educational system. The focus of this story is the importance of creating equity in the system of special education.

Educational inequities in K–12 schools have long been a topic of interest to educational researchers. The literature suggests that by providing a higher-quality education to some students than to others, our educational system contributes to economic immobility and constitutes a form of institutionalized racism.

Reasons for inequities in education may include uneven distribution of funds, educational tracking systems that end up providing a higher-quality education to certain groups than to others, cultural dominance of one group over others, and discriminatory practices that provide misleading labels for many children (Delpit, 1996; Gold & Heraldo, 2012; Harry & Klingner, 2014; Kozol, 1991, 2000; Lawrence-Lightfoot, 2003; McLaren, 2003; Oakes et al., 2014).

When a child cannot obtain or make use of an education, that education is not accessible. Without access to the education that is provided, children are denied the opportunity to progress in their educational program. Access must not be dependent on serendipitous circumstances, such as the ability of parents to advocate for their child. Rather, access must be equally available to all children, regardless of their parents' capacity for advocacy and without stigmatizing labels.

Along with equal funding, culturally leveled playing fields, high-quality teaching, and nondiscriminatory practices, students who learn differently from the majority also have the right to an education that provides them with the skills and the tools to promote their academic ability without having to live with a deficit label. Unequal access to an education must become part of the well-established discourse on educational inequality.

Many factors must come into alignment to create the best environment for learning for children whose educational needs may differ from those of the majority of students. For the nine children in this study, access appeared to be dependent on economic resources, parent advocacy, and a learning environment with educational professionals who understood that different learning styles required different teaching methodologies. The difficulties these students encountered provide evidence of a system that allows access to only a few.

We know that it is possible to provide an education for all students. The Finnish model provides an example of a country that revamped its educational structure to make this commitment. Private schools by their very nature exclude students—and there are no private schools in Finland (Sahlberg, 2011). Students who are challenged by traditional methods of education, who have life circumstances that impede learning, who are victims of bias in the schools, and whose parents cannot advocate for them deserve an accessible education. Society as a whole will benefit when our educational system truly offers an opportunity for success to every student.

References

Adodo, S. O., & Agbayewa, J. O. (2011). Effect of homogenous and heterogeneous ability grouping class teaching on student's interest, attitude and achievement in integrated science. *International Journal of Psychology and Counselling, 3*(3), 48–54.

Alexander, M. (2012). *The new Jim Crow*. New York: The New Press.

Ames, C. (1992). Classrooms: Goals, structures, and student motivation. *Journal of Educational Psychology, 84*(3), 261–271.

Andreason, F. E. (2012). *Exceptional people: Lessons learned from special education survivors*. Lanham, MD: Rowman & Littlefield.

Armstrong, T. (2010). *Neurodiversity: Discovering the extraordinary gifts of autism, ADHD, dyslexia, and other brain differences*. Philadelphia: Da Capo.

Ates, S., Rasinski, T., Yildirim, K., & Yildiz, M. (2012). Perceptions of Turkish parents with children identified as dyslexic about the problems that they and their children experience. *Reading Psychology*, 33(5), 399–422.

Ayers, W. (2001). *To teach: The journey of a teacher*. New York: Teachers College Press.

Baglieri, S., Bejoian, L. M., Broderick, A. A., Connor, D. J., & Valle, J. (2011). [Re]claiming "Inclusive Education" toward cohesion in educational reform: Disability studies unravels the myth of the normal child. *Teachers College Record, 113*(10), 2122–2154.

Ball, E. W., & Harry, B. (2010). Assessment and the policing of the norm. In C. Dudley-Marling & A. Gurn (Eds.), *Myth of the normal curve* (pp. 105–122). New York: Peter Lang.

Balu, R., Zhu, P., Doolittle, R., Schiller, E., Jenkins, J., & Gersten, R. (2015). Evaluation of response to intervention practices for elementary school reading executive summary. National Center for Educational Evaluation and Regional Assistance.

Bandura, A. (1997). *Self-efficacy: The exercise of control*. New York: W.H. Freeman.

Barth, R. S. (1990). *Improving schools from within: Teachers, parents, and principals can make the difference*. San Francisco: Jossey-Bass.

Bird, J. M., & Bassin, S. (2015). Examining disproportionate representation in special education, disciplinary practices, and the School-to-Prison Pipeline II. *Communique* (5), 1.

Bourdieu, P. (1977). Cultural reproduction and social reproduction. In J. Karabel & A. Halsey (Eds.), *Power and ideology in education* (pp. 487–511). New York: Oxford University Press.

Bourdieu, P., & Wacquant, L. (1992). *An invitation to reflexive sociology*. Chicago: University of Chicago Press.

Büttner, G., & Hasselhorn, M. (2011). Learning disabilities: Debates on definitions, causes, subtypes, and responses. *International Journal of Disability, Development & Education, 58*(1), 75–87.

Campbell-Whatley, G., & Lyons, J. (2013). *Leadership practices for special and general educators*. Boston: Pearson.

Cochran-Smith, M., & Lytle, S. (1993). *Inside/outside: Teacher research and knowledge*. New York: Teachers College Press.

Crawford, F. A., & Bartolome, L. (2010). Labeling and treating linguistic minority students with disabilities as deficient and outside the normal curve: A pedagogy of exclusion. In C. Dudley-Marling & A. Gurn (Eds.), *The myth of the normal curve* (pp. 151–170). New York: Peter Lang.

Crouch, E. R. & Pataki, C. (2016). Reading learning disorder follow-up. *Medscape*. Retrieved from http://emedicine.medscape.com/article/1835801-followup.

Darling-Hammond, L. (1997). *The right to learn: A blueprint for creating schools that work*. San Francisco: Jossey-Bass.

Darling-Hammond, L. (2004). "Separate but equal" to "No Child Left Behind": The collision of new standards and old inequalities. In D. Meier & G. Wood (Eds.), *Many children left behind* (pp. 3–32). Boston: Beacon Press.

Davies, D. (2002). The 10th school revisited: Are school/family/community partnerships on the reform agenda now? *Phi Delta Kappan, 83*(5), 388–392.

Deal, T. E., & Peterson, K. D. (1990). *The principal's role in shaping school culture*. Washington, DC: Office of Educational Research and Improvement.

Deal, T. E., & Peterson, K. D. (1999). *Shaping school culture: The heart of leadership*. San Francisco: Jossey-Bass.

Definition of dyslexia (n.d.). Retrieved October 7, 2016, from https://dyslexiaida.org/definition-of-dyslexia.

Delpit, L. (1996). *Other people's children: Cultural conflict in the classroom*. New York: New Press.

DePlanty, J., Coulter-Kern, R., & Duchane, K. (2007). Perceptions of parent involvement in academic achievement. *Journal of Educational Research, 100*(6), 361–367.

Dudley-Marling, C., & Gurn, A. (2010). Introduction: Living on the boundaries of normal. In C. Dudley-Marling & A. Gurn (Eds.), *The myth of the normal curve* (pp. 1–8). New York: Peter Lang.

Epstein, J. (1987). What principals should know about parent involvement. *Principal Leadership, 66*, 6–9.

Ferri, B. (2010). A dialogue we've yet to have: Race and disability studies. In C. Dudley-Marling & A. Gurn (Eds.), *The myth of the normal curve* (pp. 139–150). New York: Peter Lang.

Ferris, S. (2015). *An epidemic of questionable arrests by school police*. Washington, DC: The Center for Public Integrity. Retrieved from https://www.publicintegrity.org/2015/12/10/18944/epidemic-questionable-arrests-school-police.

Fletcher, J. M., Lyon, G. R., Fuchs, L. S., & Barnes, M. A. (2007). *Learning disabilities: From identification to intervention*. New York: Guilford Press.

Frankel, H. (2009). A child with a dyslexia diagnosis gets extra classroom support. Are canny parents playing the system? *Times Educational Supplement* (4833), 10–17.

Fuchs, L. S., Fuchs, D., Compton, D. L., Wehby, J., Schumacher, R. F., Gersten, R., & Jordan, N. C. (2015). Inclusion versus specialized intervention for very-low-performing students: What does access mean in an era of academic challenge? *Exceptional Children* (2), 134. doi: 10.1177/0014402914551743.

Fullan, M., & Hargreaves, A. (1996). *What's worth fighting for in your school*. New York: Teachers College Press.

Gabrieli, J. D. E. (2009). Dyslexia: A new synergy between education and cognitive neuroscience. *Science, 325*(5938), 280–283.

Gallagher, D. (2010). Educational researchers and the making of normal people. In C. Dudley-Marling & A. Gurn (Eds.), *The myth of the normal curve* (pp. 25–38). New York: Peter Lang.

Gasbarra, P., Johnson, J., & Public, A. (2008). A matter of trust: Ten key insights from recent public opinion research on attitudes about education among Hispanic parents, students and young adults: Public Agenda. Retrieved August 2011 from http://www.publicagenda.org.

Gelb, S. (2010). Evolutionary anxiety, monstrosity, and the birth of normality. In C. Dudley-Marling & A. Gurn (Eds.), *The myth of the normal curve* (pp. 71–86). New York: Peter Lang.

Gold, M. E., & Heraldo, R. (2012). To Label or not to label: The special education question for African Americans. *Educational Foundations, 26*(1-2), 143–156.

Grigorenko, E. L., Macomber, D., Hart, L., Naples, A., Chapman, J., Geib, C. F., & Wagner, R. (2015). Academic achievement among juvenile detainees. *Journal of Learning Disabilities, 48*(4), 359.

Gulamhussein, A. (2013). *Teaching the teachers: Effective professional development in the era of high stakes accountability.* Alexandria, VA: The Center for Public Education.

Gurn, A. (2010). Conclusion: Re/visioning the ideological imagination of (special) education. In C. Dudley-Marling & A. Gurn (Eds.), *The myth of the normal curve* (pp. 241–255). New York: Peter Lang.

Harry, B., & Klingner, J. (2014). *Why are so many minority students in special education? Understanding race and disability in schools* (2nd ed.). New York: Teachers College Press.

Hart-Tervalon, D., & Garcia, D. (2014). Educational systems change at the state level. In Kozleski, E. B., & Thorius, K. K. (Eds.), *Ability, equity, and culture: Sustaining inclusive urban education reform* (pp. 199–216). New York: Teachers College Press.

Herzik, L. (2015). A better IDEA: Implementing a nationwide definition for significant disproportionality to combat overrepresentation of minority students in special education. *San Diego Law Review, 52*(4), 951–966.

Hoeft, F., Hernandez, A., McMillon, G., Taylor-Hill, H., Martindale, J. L., & Meyler, A. (2006). Neural basis of dyslexia: A comparison between dyslexic and nondyslexic children equated for reading ability. *Journal of Neuroscience, 26*(42), 10700–10708.

Hopson, L., & Lawson, H. (2011). Social workers' leadership for positive school climates via data-informed planning and decision making. *Children & Schools, 33*(2), 106–118.

Howard, E. (2015). *African American parents' perceptions of public school: African American parents' involvement in their childrens' educations.* Johnson City, TN: East Tennessee State University.

Ketterlin-Geller, L. R., Baumer, P., & Lichon, K. (2015). Administrators as advocates for teacher collaboration. *Intervention in School and Clinic, 51*(1), 51–57.

Kim, S. W., & Hill, N. E. (2015). Including fathers in the picture: A meta-analysis of parental involvement and students' academic achievement. *Journal of Educational Psychology, 107*(4), 919–934.

Kirk, J., & Reid, G. (2001). An examination of the relationship between dyslexia and offending in young people and the implications for the training system. *Dyslexia 7*(2), 77–84.

Kozol, J. (1991). *Savage inequalities: Children in America's schools.* New York: Crown.

Kozol, J. (2000). An unequal education. *School Library Journal, 46*(5), 46–49. Retrieved January 6, 2010, from ERIC database.

Ladson-Billings, G. (2006). From the achievement gap to the education debt: Understanding achievement in U.S. schools. *Educational Researcher, 35*(7), 3.

Lapkin, E. (2014). Dyslexia by the Numbers. Retrieved from https://www.understood.org/en/learning-attention-issues/child-learning-disabilities/dyslexia/dyslexia-by-the-numbers.

Lareau, A., & Horvat, E. M. (1999). Moments of social inclusion and exclusion: Race, class, and cultural capital in family-school relationships. *Sociology of Education, 72*(1), 37–53.

Lavoie, R. (2008). The teacher's role in home/school communication: Everybody wins. Retrieved from http://www.ldonline.org/article/28021.

Lawrence-Lightfoot, S. (2003). *The essential conversation: What parents and teachers can learn from each other.* New York: Random House.

Lee, J. (2002). Racial and ethnic achievement gap trends: Reversing the progress toward equity? *Educational Researcher, 31*(1), 3–12.

Lewis, A., & Diamond, J. (2015). *Despite the best intentions: How racial inequality thrives in good schools.* New York: Oxford Press.

Lieberman, A., & Miller, L. (2008). Developing capacities. In A. Lieberman & L. Miller (Eds.), *Teachers in professional communities* (pp. 18–28). New York: Teachers College Press.

Losen, D. J., Ee, J., Hodson, C., & Martinez, T. (2015). Disturbing inequities: Exploring the relationship between racial disparities in special education identification and discipline. In D. Losen (Ed.), *Closing the school discipline gap: Equitable remedies for excessive exclusion* (pp. 89–106). New York: Teachers College Press.

Lyon, G. R., Sally, E. S., & Bennett, A. S. (2003). Defining dyslexia, comorbidity, teachers' knowledge of language and reading a definition of dyslexia. *Annals of Dyslexia, 53,* 1.

Maccartney, B. (2010). Living on the edge of the normal curve: It's like a smack in the head. In C. Dudley-Marling & A. Gurn (Eds.), *The myth of the normal curve* (pp. 205–220). New York: Peter Lang.

Macedo, D., & Marti, T. S. (2010). Situating labeling within an ideological framework. In C. Dudley-Marling & A. Gurn (Eds.), *The myth of the normal curve* (pp. 53–70). New York: Peter Lang.

Maehr, M. L., & Midgley, C. (1996). *Transforming school cultures.* Boulder, CO: Westview Press.

Mapp, K. (2003). Having their say: Parents describe how and why they are involved in their children's education. *School Community Journal, 13*(1), 35–64.

McLaren, P. (2003). *Life in schools: An introduction to critical pedagogy in the foundations of education.* Boston: Pearson Education.

Mclaughlin, M., & Talbert, J. (2001). *Professional communities and the work of high school teaching.* Chicago: University of Chicago Press.

Meier, D. (2002). *In schools we trust: Creating communities of learning in an era of testing and standardization.* Boston: Beacon Press.

Moats, L. C., & Dakin, K. E. (2016). Dyslexia Basics. Retrieved from http://dyslexiaida.org/dyslexia-basics/.

Moody, K., Holzer, C., Roman, M., Freeman, D., Haynes, M., & James, T. (2000). Prevalence of dyslexia among Texas prison inmates. *Texas Medicine, 96*(6), 69–75.

Morgan, P. L., Farkas, G., Hillemeier, M. M., Mattison, R., Maczuga, S., Li, H., & Cook, M. (2015). Minorities are disproportionately underrepresented in special education: Longitudinal evidence across five disability conditions. *Educational Researcher, 44*(5), 278–292.

Nord, C., & West, J. (2001). Factors associated with fathers' and mothers' involvement in their children's schools. *Education Statistics Quarterly, 3*(2), 40–43.

Nugent, M. (2008). Services for children with dyslexia—the child's experience. *Educational Psychology in Practice, 24*(3), 189–206.

Oakes, J. (1985, 2005). *Keeping track: How schools structure inequality.* New Haven, CT: Yale University Press.

Oakes, J., Lipton, M., Anderson, L., & Stillman, J. (2014). *Teaching to change the world.* New York: Teachers College Press.

Olson, K. (2009). *Wounded by school: Recapturing the joy in learning and standing up to old school culture.* New York: Teachers College Press.

Petteruti, A., Schindler, M., & Ziedenberg, J. (2014). *Sticker shock: Calculating the full price tag for youth incarceration.* Washington, DC: Justice Policy Institute.

Pritchard, R. R. (2012). *The influence of ability grouping on math achievement in a rural middle school.* South Orange, NJ: Seton Hall University. Retrieved from http://scholarship.shu.edu/cgi/viewcontent.cgi?article=2824&context=dissertations.

Pullen, P. (2016). Historical and current perspectives on learning disabilities in the united states. *Learning Disabilities: A Contemporary Journal, 14*(1), 25–37.

Rathyen, C. (2004). Providing safety in a multi-cultural, multi-ability classroom. *Delta Kappa Gamma Bulletin, 71*(1), 52–55.

Reiff, M., & Ballin, A. (2016). Adult Graduate Student Voices. *Adult Learning, 27*(2), 76–83.

Renchler, R. (1992). Student motivation, school culture, and academic achievement: What school leaders can do. *Trends and Issues paper. ERIC Clearinghouse on Educational Management. (ERIC Document No. ED351741).* Retrieved May 1, 2008, from ERIC database.

Rogers, R., & Mancini, M. (2010). Requires medication to progress academically: The discursive pathways of ADHD. In C. Dudley-Marling & A. Gurn (Eds.), *The myth of the normal curve* (pp. 87–104). New York: Peter Lang.

Ronfeldt, M., Farmer, S. O., McQueen, K., & Grissom, J. A. (2015). Teacher collaboration in instructional teams and student achievement. *American Educational Research Journal, 52*(3), 475.

Rozalski, M., Stewart, A., & Miller, J. (2010). How to determine the least restrictive environment for students with disabilities. *Exceptionality, 18*(3), 151–163.

Sahlberg, P. (2011). *Finnish lessons: What can the world learn from educational change in Finland?* New York: Teachers College Press.

Sailor, W. (2015). Advances in schoolwide inclusive school reform. *Remedial & Special Education, 36*(2), 94–99.

Salend, S. J. (2016). *Creating inclusive classrooms: Effective, differentiated, and reflective practices.* Boston, MA: Pearson.

Sarason, S. B. (1996). *Revisiting the culture of the school and the problem of change.* New York: Teachers College Press.

Schein, E. H. (2004). *Organizational culture and leadership.* San Francisco: Jossey-Bass.

Schwarz, P. (2006). *From disability to possibility: The power of inclusive classrooms.* Portsmouth, NH: Heinemann.

Sergiovanni, T. (1994). *Building community in schools.* San Francisco: Jossey-Bass.

Shaywitz, S. (2003). *Overcoming dyslexia: A new and complete science-based program for reading problems at any level.* New York: Vintage Books.

Shulman, L. (2004). *The wisdom of practice: Essays on teaching, learning, and learning to teach.* San Francisco: Jossey-Bass.

Snowling, M. J., Adams, J. W., Bowyer-Crane, C., & Tobin, V. (2000). Levels of literacy among juvenile offenders: The incidence of specific reading difficulties. *Criminal Behaviour & Mental Health, 10*(4), 229.

Spindler, G. (Ed.). (1982). *Doing the ethnography of schooling: Educational anthropology in action.* New York: Holt, Rinehart and Winston.

Stanley, S. G. (2015). The Advocacy Efforts of African American Mothers of Children with Disabilities in Rural Special Education: Considerations for School Professionals. *Rural Special Education Quarterly, 34*(4), 3–17.

Stephanie, S. D., Adam, K. W., David, B. G., Elizabeth, M. A., et al. (2006). Suicidality, school dropout, and reading problems among adolescents. *Journal of Learning Disabilities, 39*(6), 507–515. Retrieved January 6, 2010, from ProQuest database.

Svensson, I., Lundberg, I., & Jacobson, C. (2001). The prevalence of reading and spelling difficulties among inmates of institutions for compulsory care of juvenile delinquents. *Dyslexia (10769242), 7*(2), 62–76.

Toldson, I. A., & Lemmons, B. P. (2013). Social demographics, the school environment, and parenting practices associated with parents' participation in schools and academic success among black, hispanic, and white students. *Journal of Human Behavior in the Social Environment, 23*(2), 237–255.

Valencia, R. (Ed.). (1997). *The evolution of deficit thinking: Educational thought and practice.* London: Falmer.

Wehlage, G. G., Newmann, F. M., & Secada, W. G. (1996). Standards for authentic achievement and pedagogy. In F. M. N. & Associates (Eds.), *Authentic Achievement: Restructuring schools for intellectual quality* (pp. 21–48). San Francisco: Jossey-Bass Publishers.

Williams, J., Pazey, B., Fall, A. M., Yates, J. R., & Roberts, G. J. (2015). Avoiding the threat: An exploratory study into a theoretical understanding of the de facto segregation of students with disabilities. *NASSP Bulletin, 99*(3), 233–253.

Willis, A. I. (2010). Miner's canaries and boiling frogs: Fiction and facts about normalcy in educational and reading assessment. In C. Dudley-Marling & A. Gurn (Eds.), *The myth of the normal curve* (pp. 123–138). New York: Peter Lang.

Wolf, M. (2007). *Proust and the squid: The story and science of the reading brain.* New York: Harper Collins.

Wright, P. W. & Wright, P. D. (2015). *Special Education Law* (2nd ed.). Hartfield, VA: Harbor House Law Press.

Youn, T. K. (2015). Schooling and pathways to power and privilege of generations of the best and the brightest in the American meritocracy. *Conference Papers—American Sociological Association*, 1–48.

Zernike, K. (2016, April 5). Rejected by colleges, SAT and ACT gain high school acceptance. *New York Times*. Retrieved from http://www.nytimes.com/2016/04/06/us/act-and-sat-find-a-profitable-market-as-common-core-tests.html.

Index

About the Author

Amy Ballin is currently an associate professor of practice at Simmons College in Boston, Massachusetts. She is a licensed social worker and an educator who has worked for decades in public and private schools as a teacher and a school counselor. She resides in Massachusetts with her family, dogs, chickens, and bees.

Made in the USA
Lexington, KY
11 January 2017